MYSTERY FEAST

THE MEAL OF RELEASE

WENDY VARGA

WENDY VARGA
MINISTRIES

Thoughts from the Designer about the Cover

I wanted to create a cover that would portray the Living Wine. A cup of blessing with swirls of red represent the life contained in His blood. I have been a Christian my entire life, born into a family that served God. Since a young age, I was taught the power in Communion and the life that it brings. So, when I was asked to design a cover for Wendy's book, I was ecstatic that I had the opportunity to be a part of what she is doing, spreading the real truth about Communion and the power that it holds.

Jevon Varga

Book Cover and Branding for Wendy Varga designed by:

Mystery Feast

THE MEAL OF RELEASE

WENDY VARGA

◆ FriesenPress

Suite 300 - 990 Fort St
Victoria, BC, V8V 3K2
Canada
www.friesenpress.com

ISBN
978-1-5255-2221-5 (Hardcover)
978-1-5255-2222-2 (Paperback)
978-1-5255-2223-9 (eBook)

1. RELIGION/CHRISTIAN LIFE/INSPIRATIONAL

Distributed to the trade by The Ingram Book Company

Dedication

I dedicate this book to every firstborn father and son

... and ...

to those who love them!

Author's Personal Note: During the writing of this manuscript, I was working on a project alongside my brother, brother-in-law, son, and son-in-law. I realized in amazement that they are all firstborn sons—deeply respected, deeply needed, deeply loved. This book had already been dedicated, but the new awareness staggered me. Reality of the following story suddenly became much more personal and intense. Therefore, this book is dedicated with increased passion to all firstborns everywhere and to everyone affected by their lives—in essence, the entire world.

Special Acknowledgment

With overwhelming thankfulness to the Passover Lamb Who so passionately traded places with me—securing my release.

To Him who loves us and released us from our sins by His blood—
Revelation 1:5 (NASB)

Acknowledgments

With thankfulness to my parents, Moses & Rosemary Sabo, and my parents-in-law, Peter & Katie Varga, who faithfully made sure that the blood of the Passover Lamb—Jesus Christ—was applied to their homes and the hearts of their children. Thank you for investing your lives into us!

With thankfulness to the love of my life, Michael Varga, who has faithfully stood at my side through the years. Thank you for standing with me so, together, we can invest in our children—that the power of this Meal can be revealed to coming generations.

Dear Reader

May you apprehend the Mystery in the Meal

… and …

become a steward of that Mystery!

Endorsements

Reading this manuscript as a minister, every page is sermon material! What a treasure! So amazingly put together for us by the author, the laid-out plan of God comes alive—all that was wrought for me and you, personally and intimately, through the receiving of communion. This detailed book is a wonderful walk through scripture, opening up the revelation of what we actually celebrate at this table set by God. You'll never look at the Eucharist the same again! This is not a book to read in just one sitting. This is a book to study. In doing so, your spiritual life will be truly enriched, your victory and thanksgiving truly increased. What a Saviour!!

—Pastor Eve Bassett
Lead Pastor, The Church of Abundant Life Ministries

Wendy's book is profoundly insightful and kept me hungry for more. Each chapter is a new invitation to sit with God and share a meal together.

—Grant M. Derkatz, N.H.P.

Wendy Varga uncovers multi-dimensional insight into familiar Bible passages, shedding light on the mysteries of communion. The unveiled truths provide fresh impact and personal application that inspire the reader's heart with this powerful provision of a loving and wise God.

—Debbie Hiatt
President, High Gate Press, LLC

What an accomplishment, to have finished a manuscript on a topic that is so important to those who are members of the Christian faith. Well-organized and thorough ... It's an interesting and insightful analysis and discussion of the Passover and Communion, one that I hope will help others on their journey of faith.

—Laura Matheson
Editor

MYSTERY

musterion

SACRED SECRET

Table of Contents

...I have food to eat that you know not of.

1. Nightmare

Would the nightmare ever end? Would the torture never stop? The harshness of their imposed bondage had progressed to downright deadly. That they still existed was entirely miraculous. Unending years of brutality and abuse had all but extinguished any hope kindled by yesteryear's glorious promises. Only the strongest hearts retained any glimmer of faith, occasionally emitting the briefest, tiniest flicker of any emotion they had left. Bricks, mortar, field work… Erecting monuments, building cities, passing seasons… Centuries of enslavement had all but destroyed them. Day after day after hellish day, death knocked at their door. Whipped, shackled, branded, oppressed; the treatment was harsh and inhumane. With weakened bodies crippled from torture and despondent spirits broken by abuse, surely death would be preferred to their life of enslavement. Debilitated and enfeebled by the nightmarish torture, how could they know that … *tomorrow*, everything would be different!

Tomorrow?! Oh, it was so close, yet so far away! From the very inception of their slavery, nothing eased their servitude. In fact, every attempt for relief invariably increased the torment. How could tomorrow be any different? What could possibly differentiate tomorrow from today?

Gathering together, the oppressed company met with their leader. Their morale plummeted upon hearing his words. Tonight, they were to eat supper; then … deliverance would surely arrive. Supper?! How could a mere meal change their circumstances when miraculous wonders had not? But the directives of a divinely designed meal continued to be laid out, causing faith to flicker yet once more. Certainly, it was the strangest dinner they had eaten to date. The strangest of meals eaten in the strangest of manners and called by the strangest of names, a name they had not heard before.

It was a meal called … PASSOVER.

2. Strange Instructions

"Kill the lamb!" This was nothing new—it seemed so usual, so ordinary. So, why did he insist on saying, "Kill the Passover"?[1] They had never called a lamb "Passover." This time must be different.

"Take hyssop and dip it in the blood. Then, smear your doorpost with the Passover's blood."[2] The instructions were getting stranger and stranger. Who would want blood smeared all over their home? It seemed so ridiculous and like so much extra work. Who would clean all these doors up? And, if the blood wasn't cleaned up, inevitably they would be overcome with insects and a putrid stench.

"Eat it with your shoes on your feet, and your staff in your hand."[3] Shoes on your feet? He, obviously, wasn't the one out there doing the work. The labor was intensive and

---

1   Exodus 12:21 "...take you a lamb according to your families, and kill the Passover."

2   Exodus 12:22 "...strike the lintel and the two side posts with the blood that is in the bason..."

3   Exodus 12:11 "And thus shall ye eat it; with your loins girded, your shoes on your feet, and your staff in your hand..."

relentless. Blistered, bloody feet welcomed any short relief from crippling, confining shoes while arms completely depleted of any strength desperately yearned to relax their grip on everything. Would they even be able to eat while holding onto walking sticks?

"No one can go out of the house until morning."[4] The strange instructions were becoming more and more irrational. Didn't he know they had an incredible amount of labor that needed to be done so they wouldn't be beaten and persecuted? On top of it all, he was the reason their workload had so drastically increased over these past weeks. Forced by whips to work faster, they could barely handle their own beatings; but, worse still, was watching their wives and children be severely abused because they couldn't meet their quotas for the day. Physically and mentally taxed to the limits, they struggled to stay in control of seething emotions.

Their frantic thoughts were interrupted by their leader's next words… "*This night* the Lord will pass through this land. The firstborn of every man, and the firstborn of every beast, will be killed—*unless* He sees the blood on your

---

4   Exodus 12:22 "…and none of you shall go out at the door of his house until the morning."

door."[5] Every thought of revolt was suddenly shattered. They knew the risk of disobedience was way too costly! Could this meal possibly contain more of heaven's power than all the previous supernatural wonders? After all, this wasn't just any other evening meal—this was PASSOVER!

Their leader continued... "You and your sons shall observe this rite forever. When your children ask you 'What does this mean?' you shall say, 'It is ... the Lord's Passover!'"[6]

His words fueled faith's dwindling flame. Reassuring promises slowly began to seep into their wounded souls. Fresh hopes of freedom and life slowly permeated their spirits restoring dead dreams. Words of entering a new land abounding with opportunities and favor ignited their hearts with fresh faith and expectancy. Surely, they would obey. The people bowed their heads and worshipped.

They were ready for ... PASSOVER.

---

5   Exodus 12:12-13 "For I will pass through the land of Egypt this night, and will smite all the firstborn in the land of Egypt, both man and beast...And the blood shall be to you for a token upon the houses where ye are: and when I see the blood, I will pass over you..."

6   Exodus 12:26-27 "...when your children shall say unto you, What mean ye by this service? That ye shall say, It is the sacrifice of the LORD'S Passover..."

3. The Stroke of Midnight

Eagerly, they waited for the tenth day of the month. Previously, they had passively witnessed the mighty hand of God at work. This time they must obey His very specific directives.

Faithfully and carefully, they followed His instructions to the letter. The perfect lamb had to be chosen for each household. Excitement increased with each passing moment as they gathered in anticipation—and trepidation. Passover preparation had begun. With every home affected and no age excluded, fathers carefully examined the flocks as only a spotless, unblemished lamb would suffice for this Passover Feast. Firstborn sons anxiously followed, hearts throbbing with indefinable dread. Mothers, grandmothers, brothers, and sisters worried about their beloved eldest son, brother, father, grandfather. Fathers and sons worked together, inspecting and re-inspecting their chosen lamb. The lives of their firstborns depended on their decision. For the next four days, they scrutinized, examined, inspected… Their lamb must be perfect!

The hour had come! Although the entire nation was responsible for killing their lambs, individual households needed to apply their personal lamb's blood to the doorpost of their home. The blood of their lamb would be the blood of their redemption. Men exhausted much strength and effort. Concentrating on the intense activities, they slaughtered lambs, built fires, and collected blood. Women and children quickly gathered the hyssop and ensured perfect preparation of this unusual meal. Each eye carefully watched as fathers meticulously applied blood to their doors. All prayed with desperation from the depths of their spirits. They could not save themselves. Only the blood of their lamb could save them.

Families solemnly gathered inside of blood-smeared doors as evening descended. In great haste, they carefully ate all of the lamb with staffs in their hands, belts fastened, and shoes on. Not one bone of this crucial meal was broken, and not one morsel of its flesh was left[7]. Knowing the awfulness of the impending judgment, each one hardly dared to move or even cast a glance at their door. Huddled together, they lovingly clasped their beloved firstborns behind red-stained doors as midnight drew near. *Would their lamb's blood truly be enough to halt death's blow?*

---

7   Numbers 9:12 "They shall leave none of it unto the morning, nor break any bone of it: according to all the ordinances of the passover they shall keep it."

At the precise stroke of midnight, the most horrified cries began! Judgment had been executed! Death's blow had been dealt! Voices rose in sheer panic and dread behind bloodless doors. The anguished wails increased as home after home after home discovered a dead son. Throughout the vast realm, there was not a house where there was not one dead.[8]

The shrieks and wails of mourners reached the ears of those huddled behind blood-smeared doors. Trembling, they began to look at each other. Could it be? Gradually, realization that death truly did "passover" them reached their hearts. Shouts and joyous laughter, as Hebrews embraced their living sons, mixed with the anguished wails of Egyptian taskmasters who held lifeless ones. Soon, one could not decipher between the sound of joy and the sound of weeping. The Passover lamb had been slain and eaten, dramatically distinguishing between those who had partaken of Passover and those who had not. Only those dwelling under the blood of the lamb were safe. The power of its life and lifeblood had graciously preserved their firstborns. That alone was enough to be grateful for, but … that was just the beginning.

---

8   Exodus 12:30 "And Pharaoh rose up in the night, he, and all his servants, and all the Egyptians; and there was a great cry in Egypt; for there was not a house where there was not one dead."

On this fourteenth day of Nisan, some 3500 years ago, Passover—the oldest Festival celebrated in the world—began. The Feast that would represent the birth of Israel as a nation had been eaten. New things were taking place. No wonder Moses instructed them that Passover's month was to become the first month of the year for them. No wonder he said it was to be the "beginning of months." Yes, Passover would signal their New Year. Yes, Passover would be their perpetual Feast. It was a new beginning—their lives were changed completely and forever.

They had partaken of PASSOVER … the Meal of Release.

4. Tomorrow

...on the morrow after the passover...
Numbers 33:3

Tomorrow had arrived. Victory, at last! It had been so long! Four hundred and thirty years, to be exact! Four hundred and thirty years to the day!

In fact, it was on the last day of the 430th year
that all the Lord's forces left the land.
Exodus 12:41 (NLT)

The horrific and intense bondage had annihilated so many. So many had died prematurely from the abuse and physical stress that had worn out their bodies. So many had died from the emotional torment. Pharaoh's murderous, merciless order had destroyed their beautiful baby sons. Supernatural wonders had been performed by God's hand. But, no plague, no sign, no wonder, no miracle had changed the ruthless heart of Pharaoh.

The entire Nile river had turned to blood at Moses' command; and every fish was dead. The most important source of their food and water was destroyed. From ponds to bath-houses, and even secluded containers—all water turned to blood. There was no water to be found anywhere in the land of Egypt.

Then came frogs, which overran the land. Frogs were in every place possible: outside and inside. There were frogs in bedrooms and on beds, frogs in kneading troughs and on bread, frogs on servants and on royalty. Anywhere and everywhere, there were frogs. Still, nothing changed.

Afterwards came the lice. Lice appeared everywhere as all the dust of the land became lice. Lice covered every man and every beast; biting, stinging, nasty lice.

Flies were the next order, swarms and swarms and swarms of them. Infestation of these loathsome creatures corrupted and ruined the land of Egypt—except in the land of Goshen, where the Hebrews dwelled. The miracle of separation or distinction began as the land of Goshen did not have one swarm of flies. Still, Pharaoh's heart was hard as stone.

The fifth plague was a contagious disease, spreading throughout all flocks in the land and severely affecting Egyptian economy. Every type of livestock in Egypt died; cattle, horses, camels, donkeys, goats, oxen, mules, and sheep. No animal was unaffected—except those owned by the Israelites. The Lord had decreed that He would make a distinction.

Subsequently, boils followed. This was a plague that now directly attacked Pharaoh's people. Inflammatory, throbbing eruptions broke out—extremely painful and completely incapacitating. Still, release was unattained.

Hail was the seventh plague. Those who now feared the words of Moses, quickly brought servants and animals in from the fields. A supernatural wonder of fire mingled with hail swept over the land leaving miles of devastation in its path. It beat down all vegetation, shattered every tree, and killed any man or beast caught in this fierce, powerful storm. Disease, death, destruction, and poverty were overtaking the land.

Next came locusts; so many that they were without number. Seemingly unleashed from the sky, they covered the earth so completely that one's eye could not even see the ground. Extensive damage to fields and vegetation had already occurred, but locusts came and devoured whatever had escaped the previous destructions. Ravaging all that was left of their food supply, this plague displayed the possibility of imminent death if Pharaoh's heart did not change.

Then darkness settled over the land—a darkness so thick it could be felt. Although it was only a foreshadow of their deadest, darkest night yet ahead, the palpable blackness enveloped them in a suffocating embrace of fear for three solid days. But there was light in the land of Goshen, displaying another demonstration of distinction.

Nine supernatural wonders of the world had occurred in one nation within a short time span. Virtually all Egyptian animals and vegetation were consumed by the previous plagues; but … one final, devastating judgment would yet descend. It was the death of every firstborn son and every firstborn beast. It was to occur at midnight.

But before midnight came … PASSOVER. Now came the time when they would eat the strangest of meals in the strangest of manners. This meal of divine design was their way of escape from judgment and captivity. **The flesh and blood of their perfect lamb would preserve and release them**. Not one of the previous supernatural occurrences caused a release from their bondage—*but the Feast did!* The Feast of the Passover lamb *released* them from the judgment of this last horrific plague; and *released* them from their slavery.

> *On this night the Lord kept his promise to bring*
> *his people out of the land of Egypt.*
> *Exodus 12:42 (NLT)*

They ate Passover, then … they were released from Egypt.

5. Release from Egypt

*...**on the morrow after the passover** the children of Israel went out with a high hand...*
Numbers 33:3 (NKJV)

The Israelites had eaten Passover. Overnight, more supernatural occurrences happened than on all the many previous days put together. They were released from their bondage! But, they weren't just released as they were— weak, diseased, impoverished, subjugated. No! **The Meal of Release changed everything for them.** Liberated from their oppression, the Israelites exited their land of bondage as a restored, healed, and wealthy nation—overnight! Not one person was missing. Not one person was sick or weak. All were healed. Those, who yesterday were too frail to aid in Passover's preparation, were now robust and strong; miraculously able to carry the precious belongings they had accumulated just yesterday.

The Hebrew people walked out of slavery carrying with them immense wealth from their overseers and masters, given in hopes of hastening their departure. Great favor and respect were now extended by the people who had once inflicted severe pain and intense mental agony on them. Not even a dog growled at them[9] as the Egyptians urged the Israelites to leave their land as quickly as possible. Israel's triumphant mass emigration began. They crossed the border of Egypt that day—a free nation.

Just yesterday, the blood of the Passover lamb had been applied to the top frame and two side-posts of their doors.

> *They are to take some of the blood and smear it on the sides and top of the doorframes of the houses where they eat the animal.*
> *Exodus 12:7 (NLT)*

As the Israelites applied the blood of the Passover Lamb to the top and sides of their doors, they actually applied the blood in the shape of the Hebrew letter *Chet*.

Chet symbolizes life. The merciful God of Heaven had His people paint "life" on the very entrance of their homes.

---

9   Exodus 11:7 (CJB) "But not even a dog's growl will be heard against any of the people of Isra'el, neither against people nor against animals…"

But the blood on your doorposts will serve as a
***sign**, marking the houses where you are staying…*
Exodus 12:13a (NLT)

Life had been written on their homes, inscribed with
the blood of an unblemished lamb given in exchange for
the lives of their firstborn. Purchasing their pardon, it's
blood served as their atonement. The blood was a sign.
They were branded; they were marked with "life."

…When I see the blood, I will pass over you.
This plague of death will not touch you when I
strike the land of Egypt.
Exodus 12:13b (NLT)

As the death angel went through the land, the symbol
of life painted in the Passover's blood caused death to be
de-activated in that home. Moreover, life had also been
consumed by the eating of the Passover meal. Miraculously
and wondrously, their emaciated bodies transformed—
overnight. With each miracle, faith took the place of fear!
Resilience and fortitude rose up in their spirits; courage
permeated their souls.

Chet also has the numeric value of eight. Eight is
the number of grace. Eight entails the concept of new
beginnings. God had declared to Moses that this month
of Passover would become the *"beginning* of months"
for them.

This month shall be unto you the beginning of months: it shall be the first month of the year to you.

Exodus 12:2

Therefore, the month of Nisan (called Abib before the Captivity) became the first month of the ecclesiastical calendar year for the Hebrew people. "New beginnings" was shouted out from the lifeblood of their Passover lamb that night. And, new beginnings it certainly was!

For the first time ever, Passover had been consumed! Their divine meal generated divine intervention, producing *one* night of the greatest miracles in the world's history—unmatched in quantity or quality to date. An *entire nation* was given liberation, health and immense wealth—*overnight*.

Overnight, the Israelites were *released*. Released—from slavery, judgment, sickness, weakness, and poverty. It was an all-encompassing deliverance.

The unequalled, unrivalled capacity of Heaven contained and served in one earthly meal was their turning point. Heaven's protection was *released* over their homes as they applied the blood; and, Heaven's power was *released* into their beings as they ate the Lamb—an essential, vital, precious lamb called … Passover.

PASSOVER … it was their Meal of Release.

6. Release from Wilderness Wanderings

*And they did eat of the old corn of the land **on the morrow after the passover**...*
Joshua 5:11 (NKJV)

Decades later, another Nisan arrived. It was again time to eat that wonderful Passover meal.

Jubilant masses that exodused Egypt had found themselves wandering in the wilderness because of murmuring and complaining. Kept in a state of delay for forty years, the time had finally come to enter the Promised Land! They were about to step into a new beginning yet again, in the first month of their year—the beginning of months.

With Moses now dead, Joshua—ordained by God to take Moses' place—began his leadership of the Israelite nation. (In fact, Joshua was one of only two remaining from the previous generation.) God had spoken to Joshua commanding him to be strong and courageous, for the Lord would give him the very land on which his feet were treading. Fear had detained Israel for far too long. Having been one of the twelve men that scouted Canaan's land forty years earlier, Joshua was not about to have a repeat occurrence. Joshua prepared to advance. This time he *secretly* sent *two* spies to view Jericho's land.

Standing at a seemingly impassable barrier, Joshua boldly exercised his faith in God as he had seen Moses do at the Red Sea forty long years ago. As priests stepped into the Jordan river at Joshua's command, the river rolled back in a miraculous display. The Israelites again crossed over on dry ground. The only difference—forty years ago they were fleeing; now, they are advancing! Miraculously, they had arrived at Jericho—the gateway to their promised land—but there were oh so many enemies.

In military terms, they were hopelessly outclassed. Outnumbered, out-experienced, out-powered; it seemed as though it was them against the world. But their new leader understood the power of covenant and the power of obedience.

For generations, all Hebrew male babies had been circumcised at eight days old in accordance with the Abrahamic covenant. Every Israelite male who exited the land of Egypt was circumcised.

> *This is the covenant that you and your descendants must keep: Each male among you must be circumcised.*
> *Genesis 17:10 (NLT)*

But, with all the dangers they faced in their wilderness journeys, the Israelite males born after the Exodus had not been circumcised. As Joshua recounted the Lord's faithfulness and the dangers of disobedience, the young generation of Israelites obediently responded to Joshua's orders. On Jericho's plains, covenant was re-established between Israel and their God.

> *So Joshua circumcised their sons—those who had grown up to take their fathers' places—for they had not been circumcised on the way to the Promised Land.*
> *Joshua 5:7 (NLT)*

Although they had arrived in the land promised to generations of old—Abraham, Isaac, and Jacob—they had yet to attain it. But, covenant was renewed and the fourteenth of Nisan arrived! It was time to celebrate their first Passover in Canaan's land!

In Egypt, Passover had culminated in the Exodus, releasing them from bondage, disease and poverty. Now they were in Canaan, what would Passover release them from this time?

Evening came. Lambs were slaughtered. Passover was eaten. The life and new beginnings contained in the blood of the lamb was again consumed and ingested into their very beings. **What would tomorrow hold?**

On the day after Passover, on that very day,
they ate some of the produce of the land…
Joshua 5:11 (AMP)

Tomorrow had again arrived! Yet once more, the unequalled, unrivalled capacity of Heaven contained and served in one earthly meal was their turning point. Heaven's power was released into the very core of their beings! As they consumed the Passover Lamb, *release from forty years of wilderness wanderings had come*! And … with tomorrow came a *new beginning*, life in a new land.

Passover … how many miracles could one meal produce just overnight?

7. Release into the Possession of Promise

*...the manna ceased **on the morrow**...*
Joshua 5:12

On the morrow, the old ended. Israel ate something different for the first time in forty years. *After* Passover, they ate last year's corn, grown in the land of Canaan.

*And they did eat of the old corn of the land **on the morrow after the Passover**...*
Joshua 5:11

Then ... *on the morrow,* after eating old corn, the manna ceased.

*...the manna ceased **on the morrow** after they had eaten some of the old corn of the land; neither had the children of Israel manna any more; but they did eat of the fruit of the land of Canaan that year.*
Joshua 5:12

The last morning that they ate manna was the first afternoon they ate Canaan's produce. Canaan's beautiful grapes, abundant fruit, and huge vegetables would now become their fare. They had stepped into a land flowing with milk and honey, a land of exceptional bounty.

But the miracles didn't stop there! All their hopes and dreams were to be realized as God would empower Israel for a complete takeover of the Promised Land. They were about to attain possession of their promise.

> *I am Adonai your God ... I raised my hand to them, pledging to bring them out of the land of Egypt into a land I had reconnoitered for them, a land flowing with milk and honey, the most beautiful of all lands...*
> *Ezekiel 20:5-6 (CJB)*

The abundance of Canaan was to become their own. Soon they would possess...

> *...a place where there is no lack of anything that is on the earth.*
> *Judges 18:10 (NASB)*

The first Passover in Canaan generated an unprecedented meeting between Joshua and the Commander-in-Chief of Heaven's host. As Joshua fell on his face in worship, the Captain of Hosts asked Joshua to remove his shoes. Joshua obeyed!

> *The commander of the Lord's army replied, "Take off your sandals..."*
> *Joshua 5:15 (NLT)*

This was not just a random request from heaven. This was a request representing legal action. **The removal of sandals was an action symbolizing redemption and exchange of property.**

> *Now formerly in Israel this was the **custom** concerning redeeming and exchanging property. To confirm a transaction, a man pulled off his sandal and gave it to the other. This was the way of confirming and attesting in Israel.*
> *Ruth 4:7 (AMP)*

> *To make a sale legal in those days, one person would take off a sandal and give it to the other.*
> *Ruth 4:7 (CEV)*

Taking off your sandal and giving it to the redeemer of the property was a *custom*.

> Custom: unwritten rule[10]
> Custom: *Law* established practice or usage having the force of law or right.[11]

A custom is an unwritten rule! In law, a custom has the force of right.

---

10 *Oxford American Writer's Thesaurus*, (2010), s.v. "custom."

11 *New Oxford American Dictionary*, (2010), s.v. "custom."

God was calling for constitutional action. Joshua did as he was asked and removed his sandals. This act signified confirmation of an agreement—a legal agreement.

> *So, when the … relative … said to Boaz, "Buy it for yourself," he pulled off his sandal [and gave it to Boaz to confirm the agreement].*
> *Ruth 4:8 (AMP)*

In the story of Ruth, Boaz' relative removed his sandal and gave it to Boaz. Boaz then became the *redeemer*—of the property and the person. (Boaz is a type and shadow of our Redeemer and Lord.) As Boaz received the shoe, he declared,

> *Today you are witnesses that I have bought … all the property … I have also acquired Ruth the Moabite … as my wife…*
> *Ruth 4:9-10a (NIV)*

> *…This will keep the property in his family's name, and he will be remembered in this town.*
> *Ruth 4:10b (CEV)*

Joshua removed his sandals in obedience to the all-powerful Commander-in-Chief's request; thereby sealing a covenantal, constitutional agreement with God. This act stated that God was to be the *Redeemer*. Canaan would forever be the Lord's land.

...This will keep the property in his family's name, and he will be remembered in this town.
Ruth 4:10b (CEV)

Joshua's humble obedience generated an amazing gift of bestowment.

...the Lord said to Joshua, "I have given you Jericho, its king, and all its strong warriors."
Joshua 6:2 (NLT)

God would redeem the land. **There was about to be an exchange of property**! In God's usual, supernatural, spectacular way—the way of miracles, signs, and wonders—Israel's conquest of their promise began. As trumpets blasted and people shouted, Jericho's walls came tumbling down. With the miraculous capture of the fortified city, Joshua made a riveting statement...

*...the city shall be **accursed**, even it, and all that are therein, to the LORD:*
Joshua 6:17

Accursed is the Hebrew word [cherem] meaning: dedicated thing, devoted thing, things which should have been utterly destroyed.

This Hebrew term refers to **the complete consecration of things or people to the Lord, *EITHER* by giving them as an offering *OR* by destroying them completely**. Therefore, see this verse in a different translation...

*And the city and all that is in it shall be **devoted to the Lord**...*
Joshua 6:17 (AMP, parallel Bible)

Removal of Joshua's sandals indicated redemption or exchange. Fulfilling their legal agreement, God transferred Jericho's property to the Israelites in just seven days; in turn, Joshua devoted Jericho to the Lord.

Jericho means: place of fragrance.[12] The land abounded in balsam, cyprus, honey, roses and many other fragrant products that produced beautifully pleasant aromas. Now even more beautiful fragrances ascended to the God of Heaven, fragrances of Passover's sacrificed lambs, blood-covenant, and obedience.

From Jericho, a harlot named Rahab was redeemed. Rahab, as part of the city, was also *"devoted to the Lord,"*[13] but not through destruction (like the rest of Jericho). Rahab was devoted through **complete consecration** to God. In fact, Rahab became the mother of Boaz, who was the great-grandfather of King David. She was preserved (devoted) to become part of the lineage of Jesus Christ.

---

12   "Easton's Bible Dictionary," *SwordSearcher*, iPhone ed., v. 3.4 (Brandon Staggs, 1999).

13   Joshua 6:17 "...only Rahab the harlot shall live, she and all that are with her in the house, because she hid the messengers that we sent."

*This is the genealogy of **Jesus** the Messiah **the son of David**, the son of Abraham:*
Matthew 1:1 (NIV)

*Salmon was the father of Boaz (whose mother was **Rahab**). Boaz was the father of Obed (whose mother was Ruth). Obed was the father of Jesse. Jesse was the father of King David...*
Matthew 1:5-6 (NLT)

So, from Jericho emerged another fragrance. Rahab became an ancestor of One Who would deliver the Fragrance of Life to the world.

Jesus Christ—the *fragrant* Rose of Sharon.
Jesus Christ—the *fragrant* Lily of the Valley.
Jesus Christ—the *fragrant* offering of a
perfect sacrifice.

...Christ also loved you and gave Himself up for us, an offering and sacrifice to God ... a sweet fragrance.
Ephesians 5:2 (AMP)

And, Life's sweet fragrance would be infused into His beloved church, causing us to diffuse and release His aroma to the world.

But thanks be to God, who ... uses us to spread the aroma of the knowledge of him everywhere. For we are to God the pleasing aroma of Christ

among those who are being saved and those who are perishing.
2 Corinthians 2:14-15 (NIV)

Jesus Christ would one day re-visit Jericho's plains performing the miracle of giving sight, and salvation, to blind Bartimaeus before making His Triumphal Entry into Jerusalem commissioned to *redeem some property and acquire His Bride*!

Passover on Jericho's plains released Heaven's power of protection—and the manifestation of Heaven's War General. The possessing of their promise began ... *after* Passover.

The life-giving, nation-changing, wealth-exchanging power of the Passover lamb surged through their bodies.

PASSOVER was consumed ... the meal of mysterious power, the Meal of Release!

8. Release into My Father's Business

After Passover...
Luke 2:43 (CEV)

Many centuries later, a new ecclesiastical year for the nation of Israel began. Anticipation grew as they began preparing for the fourteenth of Nisan. By the tenth day of this New Year, a perfect lamb had to be chosen, then undergo four days of examination to affirm its perfection.

With Passover being one of Israel's three Feasts that every male was expected to attend, the nation was headed to Jerusalem. (This Passover is the first encounter we have with Jesus, other than His birth; and is also the only account we have of Him between infancy and adulthood.) Jesus headed to the nation's capital with Mary and Joseph.

On the brink of manhood, He arrived in Jerusalem to celebrate and consume Passover's Feast. Passover—a new beginning was about to take place! Now twelve years old, Jesus was at a crucial age for every Jewish boy. Jewish boys would formally become a *bar mitzvah* by the end of their twelfth year. Bar Mitzvah literally means: son of commandment.

Prior to reaching bar mitzvah age, the child's parents hold the responsibility for the child's actions. After this age, the boys and girls bear their own responsibility for Jewish ritual law, tradition, and ethics, and are able to participate in all areas of Jewish community life.[14]

A Jewish boy's twelfth year was his final year of preparation before he would fully participate in synagogue life. For twelve years, Joseph had faithfully taught Jesus about the Jewish commandments, laws, and rituals. Time drew near for Jesus to bear greater responsibility.

On Passover Day, at the ninth hour (3:00 pm), the sacrifice began. Jesus watched as Joseph slaughtered the family's lamb alongside thousands of other fathers. Did He know that soon *He* would be Passover's Lamb?

While consuming Passover's meal that evening, Jewish children asked the ceremonial question,

> *"Why are we doing these things?..."*
> *Exodus 12:26 (EXB)*

The story of God's deliverance was once again told to the next generation. Joseph responded to Jesus' question with the all-familiar story of Heaven's unrivalled, unequalled power that moved on their behalf. It was a

---

14   Wikipedia, s.v. "Bar and Bat Mitzvah." https://en.wikipedia.org/wiki/Bar_and_Bat_Mitzvah

fervent, passionate account of their release from Egypt. The memories of incredible deliverance had not faded.

> *...And you will reply, 'It is the Passover sacrifice to the Lord, for he passed over the houses of the Israelites in Egypt. And though he struck the Egyptians, he spared our families.'...*
> Exodus 12:27 (NLT)

This brought to remembrance so many more accounts of God's mystical, miraculous power; a power generated by Israel's obedience in commemorating the Passover Feast.

> ➢ Passover on the plains of Jericho
> ➢ the exceptional Passover Feast held by King Josiah
> ➢ Passover celebrated by King Hezekiah after cleansing the Temple
> ➢ Passover kept by the children of the captivity during the days of Ezra.

Passover—it was a history of supernatural! What a precious Meal this had become! God had shown them time and time again that He supersedes every government and kingdom of this world! His mighty acts demonstrated His ability to supersede every power that ever was and every power that ever will be! After all, He is God!

> *...God, supreme over the nations, supreme over the earth.*
> Psalm 46:11 (CJB)

The Passover stories of God's redemptive acts caused Jesus' heart to overflow with faith in His Heavenly Father. Every account Joseph told increased their faith, intensified their passion, and filled their hearts with joy as the Festival drew to a close. *Tomorrow*, they would begin their journey home. Tomorrow … what would tomorrow hold?

> ***After the festival was over***, *while his parents were returning home, the boy Jesus stayed behind in Jerusalem…*
> Luke 2:43 (NIV)

Joseph and Mary headed back to Nazareth with family and friends, relishing memories of the chaotically busy, yet glorious time in Jerusalem. Jerusalem to Nazareth, it was a journey that required much energy. Joyous chatter dwindled, exhaustion took over, and weary travellers gradually wandered back to their families.

Where is Jesus? Joseph and Mary began to wonder. Night descended as they searched for him among the travellers, but He was nowhere to be found. Stark reality that Jesus was not with them sank into their spirits. He was very nearly a *bar mitzvah*, a son of commandment. Obedience was His outstanding trait. Where could he be? They had looked everywhere. Could he still be in the City of Jerusalem? Jerusalem seemed to be the only option left.

Gripped by fear, Joseph and Mary turned around. Praying with desperation, they headed back to Jerusalem. The light-heartedness of their morning had turned into bitter anguish of the heart. For three days, they anxiously scoured Jerusalem. How would they find their twelve-year-old son in a city still overcrowded with Passover worshippers?

Deep distress permeated Mary's heart! Fear and concern choked her spirit. With ever-increasing self-examination, the questions just would not relent. Was her assignment as "mother of the Messiah" over? Jesus was the very Son of God, she knew that better than anyone. The day the angel Gabriel came to her was etched deep within her memory. She remembered the shocking news that she had been chosen to carry the Messiah.[15] She remembered when the angel said that she would have a Son conceived by the Holy Spirit.[16] She remembered that He was to receive the throne of David[17] and reign over the house of Jacob.[18] And, how very well she recalled the humiliation and shame she had to endure as a scandalous story of immorality swept through a neighborhood that would not, and certainly could not, believe her. Some days she

---

15   Luke 1:31 "And, behold, thou shalt conceive in thy womb, and bring forth a son, and shalt call his name JESUS."

16   Luke 1:35 "And the angel answered and said unto her, The Holy Ghost shall come upon thee, and the power of the Highest shall overshadow thee: therefore also that holy thing which shall be born of thee shall be called the Son of God."

17   Luke 1:32 "He shall be great, and shall be called the Son of the Highest: and the Lord God shall give unto him the throne of his father David:"

18   Luke 1:33 "And he shall reign over the house of Jacob for ever; and of his kingdom there shall be no end."

could still feel the immense embarrassment and awkwardness of relatives and friends turning away in disbelief and disgust of her "condition."

Had she had failed in her duty of raising *God's Son*? This was the greatest question of all. She had faced all other circumstances head on, but how would she ever face her God?

Three days of searching, full of stress and fear—a seeming eternity. Giving up didn't really seem like an option but where else could they possibly look? Had they by-passed him somewhere on the crowded streets? Did he have enough to eat? Where was he sleeping? Was he still safe? The questions never ceased.

With every seemingly possible course of action taken, their feet and hearts grew heavier and heavier. Each step became more difficult, each thought more tormenting, each day more disparaging. How could they ever again come before God, knowing they had failed in the profound responsibilities and obligations of raising His Son? Yet, their integrity and faithfulness would not let them rest. Yes, they would head to the Temple before going home, to pray in repentance.

Sorrowful and heavy at heart, they stepped into the Temple wanting nothing more than to be inconspicuous. Famous, important Jewish teachers were still teaching many who sat around them. Amidst the rabbinical teaching style of questions and discussion, a familiar voice reached Mary's ears. This wasn't the first time during these three excruciating days that she had imagined hearing His voice. Yet ... there it was again. Could it possibly be?

> *And it came to pass, that after three days they found him in the temple, sitting in the midst of the doctors, both hearing them, and asking them questions.*
> *Luke 2:46*

Their eyes soon found the desire of their hearts! Jesus was alive and right here in the Temple!

> *When his parents saw him, they were astonished. His mother said to him, "Son, why have you treated us like this? Your father and I have been anxiously searching for you."*
> *Luke 2:48 (NIV)*

Her single question contained all the chaotic turmoil of the past three days, and even some of the past twelve years. With respect and honor, Jesus lovingly responded.

> *...How is it that you had to look for Me? Did you not see and know that it is necessary [as a duty] for Me to be ... about My Father's business?*
> *Luke 2:49 (AMP, parallel Bible)*

Just as astonished as the Jewish leaders listening to Jesus, Joseph and Mary were unable to fully comprehend their twelve-year-old's response!

> ...*they did not understand what he was saying to them.*
>
> *Luke 2:50 (NIV)*

He sat in the midst of master instructors, rabbis, and teachers of Jewish law who were discussing spiritual truths. Listening with incredible discernment and speaking with profound wisdom, His statements and questions pierced the heart of their discussions. Overwhelmed and bewildered, all who were there wondered at His understanding.[19] It was as though *overnight* Jesus had gone from being their earthly son to being about His Father's business. His Father's business—that was what He was born for! Compulsion to do His Heavenly Father's will filled the twelve-year-old.

Just three days *after* the Festival, Jesus declared to the world His new beginning. Passover had released him into His Father's business as Son of God. Completely abandoning His heart and will, He would live a life of obedience—a life fully surrendered to His Heavenly Father's **command.**

Passover ... released Him into His destined position as "Son of Commandment."

---

19   Luke 2:47 "And all that heard him were astonished at his understanding and answers."

9. Son of Commandment

After Passover, Jesus transitioned from a questioning boy to one of increasing wisdom and favor.

> *And Jesus increased in wisdom and stature, and in favour with God and man.*
> *Luke 2:52*

After Passover, Jesus subtly declared that He was on a mission of His Father's business. He was determined to live His life as a "Son of commandment."

> *For I have not spoken of myself; but the Father which sent me, he gave me a **commandment**, what I should say, and what I should speak.*
> *John 12:49 (NKJV)*

Commandment is the Greek word [entole] pronounced [en-tol-ay']. Interestingly, this word *commandment* means: **an authoritative prescription**.

A prescription is something that is prescribed to bring life and health out of sickness and pain. *Every* commandment of God is a prescription that restores life and health to our very beings. Jesus knew every commandment of God contains life.

> **I know that His commandment is eternal life**; *therefore the things I speak, I speak just as the Father has told Me.*
> *John 12:50 (NASB)*

Adhering to God's *prescriptions*, or His commandments, brings life to every area of our beings—physically, emotionally, financially, and spiritually.

> *...I know that his commandment is life...*
> *John 12:50*

> *...man lives by every word that proceeds out of the mouth of the Lord.*
> *Deuteronomy 8:3 (AMP)*

Those who disregard the commandments of God experience the downward spiral of death's power in many areas of their lives. Those who obey His commandments align themselves with life and cause a manifestation of Jesus to be their portion.

> *He that hath my commandments,* **and keepeth them***, he it is that loveth me: and he that loveth me shall be loved of my Father, and I will love him, and* **will manifest myself to him***.*
> *John 14:21*

There are different types of prescriptions. Prescriptions can relate to *health* or *property*. God's prescriptions (commandments) also encompass the same.

HEALTH PRESCRIPTION
God's Authoritative Prescription brings us relief from disease!

In regard to prescriptions related to health, there are different types of prescription drugs. These include: stimulants, painkillers, tranquilizers, and steroids.

➢ **Stimulants** treat disorders and deficits.

➢ **Painkillers** are used for the removal of pain.

➢ **Tranquilizers** are used to remove anxiety and give peace.

➢ **Steroids** treat a variety of health problems and inflammatory conditions, and also enhance performance.

What an amazing parallel to the spiritual *prescriptions* (commandments) of our Father God. Obedience to His "Authoritative Prescription" brings us every kind of health benefit.

Stimulants: His Words are like a stimulant. His words treat health disorders and deficits, rendering every disease ineffective.

> *He sent His word and healed them…*
> *Psalm 107:20*

> *… [He] healeth **all** thy diseases;*
> *Psalm 103:3*

Painkillers: His words, His commandments, are like a painkiller. No matter what causes the pain, His word brings relief from the suffering and discomfort. His word is the healing balm.

> *God said, "I've taken a good, long look at the affliction of my people … I know all about their pain. And now I have come down to help them…*
> *Exodus 3:7-8 (MSG)*

> *When the worst happens—whether war or flood or disease or famine—and we … pray out our pain and trouble, we know that you will listen and give victory.*
> *2 Chronicles 20:9 (MSG)*

Tranquilizers: His word brings relief from mental torment and anxiety—no more panic attacks, no more agitation, no more dread. Nervousness, hysteria, and phobias are all treated with God's Authoritative Prescription. His peace reassures the heart, setting up a fortress over your mind.

And the peace of God, which surpasses all com-
prehension, will guard your hearts and your
minds in Christ Jesus.
Philippians 4:7 (NASB)

…God will bless you with peace that no one
can completely understand. And this peace will
control the way you think and feel.
Philippians 4:7 (CEV)

He healeth the broken in heart…
Psalm 147:3 (NKJV)

…Behold, I give unto him my covenant of peace:
Numbers 25:12 (NKJV)

Peace I leave with you; my peace I give you. I
do not give to you as the world gives. Do not let
your heart be troubled and do not be afraid.
John 14:27 (NIV)

Steroids: Just like steroids, God's word treats a variety of inflammatory conditions and enhances performance. Every festering, inflamed wound from infectious causes—to body or soul—is soothed and comforted by the fragrant ointment of His Word. His Word brings strength and fortitude to our bodies, minds and spirits.

He … bindeth up their wounds.
Psalm 147:3

Now look at me: God has kept me alive, as he promised ... here I am today, eighty-five years old! I'm as strong as I was the day Moses sent me out. I'm as strong as ever in battle, whether coming or going.
Joshua 14:10-11 (MSG)

...let the weak say, I am strong.
Joel 3:10

...be strong, all you people of the land ... For I am with you, declares the LORD Almighty.
Haggai 2:4 (NIV)

Finally, my brethren, be strong in the Lord, and in the power of his might.
Ephesians 6:10

...but the people that do know their God shall be strong, and do exploits.
Daniel 11:32

God's prescription for health and wholeness is in His every command. Following His prescription leads to recovery, health, strength, and life—enhancing our performance.

PROPERTY PRESCRIPTION
God's Authoritative Prescription brings us relief from lack!

Prescription is also a legal term that applies to property. Here are some definitions of prescription relating to property.

> Prescription is the process of acquiring rights and in particular *obtaining a good title to land* as a result of the passage of time.[20]

> ...prescription relates to a right to use the *property* of another that is consistent with the rights of the owner.[21]

God commanded Israel to...

> ... *ask their Egyptian neighbors for articles of silver and gold.*
> *Exodus 11:2 (NLT)*

> *So the people of Israel did just as the Lord had commanded...*
> *Exodus 12:28 (NLT)*

---

20   "Acquiring rights to land by way of prescription," *TCY Legal Chit Chat.* http://www.tcyoung.co.uk/blog/2012/commercial/acquiring-rights-to-land-by-way-of-prescription

21   *The Free Dictionary,* "Prescription." http://legal-dictionary.thefreedictionary.com/prescription

As Israel *obeyed* God, Egypt's wealth was transferred to them.

Taking a prescription is necessary in order to receive the benefits of it. Therefore, in order to receive the benefits of God's Authoritative Prescription, you must "fill" the order and take it. In other words—obey.

> ...*there shall be no poor among you* ... **Only if** thou carefully hearken unto the voice of the LORD thy God, to **observe to do all these commandments** which I command thee this day.
> *Deuteronomy 15:4*

Obedience to God's command also enabled Israel to acquire rights and titles to lands that had not belonged to them before.

> ...*for the LORD shall greatly bless thee in the land which the LORD thy God giveth thee for an inheritance to possess it:* **Only if** thou carefully hearken unto the voice of the LORD thy God, to **observe to do all these commandments** which I command thee this day.
> *Deuteronomy 15:4*

> As the LORD commanded Moses his servant, so did Moses command Joshua, and so did Joshua; **he left nothing undone** of all that the LORD commanded Moses.
> *Joshua 11:15 (NKJV)*

Legally, rights can be lost by not acting in a timely manner. The same is true in the spiritual realm.

> In legal terms, prescription is a rule that can cause you to gain or lose rights just by the passage of time. **To avoid losing a right, it is therefore very important to act before it is too late.**[22]

Instant obedience to God's commands results in great gain and great benefits, while delay causes loss and hardship.

Jesus had a great understanding of the power of obedience. After all, He was a "Son of commandment." He knew that His very life—and, indeed, the life of the world—depended on it.

> *And being found in fashion as a man, he humbled himself, and **became obedient**...*
> *Philippians 2:8*

"Being found in fashion as a man..." Shedding everything unlimited and immeasurable about Himself to wear the limitations of humanity, Almighty God put on the suit of a man's body. Infinite God emptied Himself to become finite man.

The God of the Universe Who spoke and hung the earth in place, breathed life into the human race, and

---

22   "Prescription: Legal Deadlines" *Éducaloi.*
https://www.educaloi.qc.ca/en/capsules/prescription-legal-deadlines

undergirds all things—*He* found Himself in the body of not just a man, but a tiny infant!

Having emptied Himself of His omniscience, Jesus knew the only way to succeed as a human was to become completely dependent upon, and obedient to, His Father's command.

**Ultimate obedience is ultimate humility
and ultimate humility is ultimate obedience.**

Jesus became obedient "even unto death." Complete, total, perfect obedience was His goal, even if it led to His demise—a cruel, agonizing, torturous death.

> *…he … became obedient unto death, even the death of the cross.*
> *Philippians 2:8 (NKJV)*

Nothing was of more importance to Jesus than ultimate obedience to His Father. Love for His Father consumed Him; and…

Love = Obedience.

Jesus was the ultimate, perfect "Son of commandment."

> ***…so that the world may know that I love the Father, I do exactly as the Father commanded Me…***
> *John 14:31 (NASB)*

10. Release into Effectual, Powerful, Authoritative Ministry

*...the Jews' passover was at hand, and Jesus went
up to Jerusalem,*
John 2:13

In the second chapter of John, we find the second recorded account of a Passover Feast celebrated by Jesus. Now a grown man, Jesus is just entering public ministry.

In John chapter one, John the Baptist is witnessing in Bethabara and baptizing in the Jordan river. John had been born to "prepare the way of the Lord" (Luke 1:76), and John's instructions from God were...

*Upon Him Whom you shall see the Spirit descend
and remain, that One is He Who baptizes with
the Holy Spirit.*
John 1:33 (AMP, parallel Bible)

As Jesus was baptized by John, John saw the foretold sign that signalled the coming of God's Son.

*...I have seen the Spirit descending as a dove out
of heaven, and it dwelt on Him ... And I have
seen [that happen—I actually did see it] and my
testimony is that this is the Son of God!*
John 1:32,34 (AMP, parallel Bible)

On two separate occasions, John the Baptist makes a statement as he sees Jesus coming toward him near the Jordan, some twenty-five miles away from Nazareth. It is a statement that will affect Passover forever...

*...Behold the **Lamb of God**, which taketh away
the sin of the world.*
John 1:29

And, again the next day...

*...Behold **the Lamb of God**!*
John 1:36

Jesus, baptized by John, already had a small following of disciples; and, although on the brink of ministry, His time had not yet arrived. Along with His mother and disciples, Jesus was invited to attend a wedding in Cana of Galilee. As the wedding ran out of wine for their guests, Mary told her Son, "They have no wine."

Jesus replied, "My hour is not yet come!" (see John 2:4).

But, Mary knew the power of obedience; after all, her Son was a "Son of *commandment.*" So, she looked over at the servants and said to them,

> *...Whatever He says to you,* ***do it.***
> *John 2:5 (AMP, parallel Bible)*

Obedience! It's a demonstration of faith and love; and it has a way of causing God to move. In fact, later in His ministry, Jesus declared that obedience causes Him to display and reveal Himself, or manifest.

> *He that hath my commandments,* ***and keepeth them [obedience*],*** *he it is that loveth me: and he that loveth me shall be loved of my Father, and I will love him,* ***and will manifest myself to him.***
> *John 14:21(NKJV) [paraphrase*: author's]*

Remember: Love = Obedience. Therefore, love can be defined as obedience. Obedience is an act of love in compliance with His command, and it causes a manifestation of Jesus.

The servant's obedience combined with Mary's faith, compelling a release of His glory and the first of many miracles to come ahead of schedule.

> ***This beginning of miracles*** *did Jesus in Cana of Galilee, and <u>manifested forth his glory</u>...*
> *John 2:11*

After this "beginning" miracle, Jesus headed to Capernaum. In just a few short days, He would be heading to Jerusalem for Passover. The Meal of Release was again about to take place. What would this Passover hold for Jesus?

> *Now when he was in Jerusalem at the passover,*
> *in the feast day,* **many believed in his name,**
> *when they saw the* **miracles** *which he did.*
> John 2:23

Passover, the Meal of Release, released Jesus into His ministry of miracles! Up until this time, He had performed only one miracle—changing water into wine. His first miracle was performed days ahead of schedule, the result of an irresistible pull of love (obedience) on His Father's heart. In Cana—one miracle took place; but, in Jerusalem, on Passover Day—miracle[s] took place.

The time had come! Passover thrust Him into His "time." Miracles flowed out of Him in a steady stream— miracles of healing, deliverance, provision, and resurrection; miracles of might and power; miracles that defied all natural laws; miracles of God's authority over earth's elements. **Miracles that showed everything Jesus does supersedes the powers of this world.**

From this Passover day forward, the life of Jesus consisted of performing miracle after miracle after miracle. Miracles of walking on water, wind and sea calmed, fig trees dried up, fish and bread multiplied, lepers cleansed, deaf ears healed, blind eyes opened, diseases cured, demons cast out, lame restored, and dead raised to life.

Passover had arrived … releasing Jesus into His effective, powerful, authoritative ministry.

11. Release of a Sacred Secret

...the passover, a feast of the Jews, was nigh.
John 6:4

For three years, Jesus continued to operate in His powerful and effective way. Countless miracles took place as Jesus Christ touched and transformed people's lives! Masses were fed, multitudes were healed, and parables were taught. With all the miracles and joy that He brought to humanity, Jesus' ministry was at an all-time high!

Witnessing some of the most amazing miracles in history, crowds followed Him everywhere He went! With unrelenting compassion, Jesus poured out love on every needy soul that sought Him. Graciously, He restored and cleansed. Never did He turn away as they asked, pleaded, shouted, begged, or cried out in desperation—even just to touch His garment. Every single person who touched Him was instantly delivered; set free from any pain or infirmity—of body or soul.

And the whole multitude sought to touch him:
for there went virtue out of him, and healed
them all.

Luke 6:19

Frantic, frenzied parents of dying children, the grievously tormented, the deaf, the mute, the lame, the blind—all desperately groped for just a single moment of His time. News of the miracles spread throughout the region quickly as futile, and even fatal, cases were restored back to perfection with just a word.

...speak the word only, and my servant shall be healed.
Matthew 8:8 (NKJV)

Every frantic cry for mercy, every radical act of faith, and every desperate grasp of His robe stirred the heart of this Miracle-worker. With compassion, He restored and transformed. Every tender touch, gentle word, and spoken blessing produced the same result—a beautiful, welcomed, delightful, life-giving miracle. Miracle, after miracle, after miracle!

...they laid the sick in the streets, and besought
him that they might touch if it were but the
border of his garment: and as many as touched
him were made whole.
Mark 6:56

...the blind and dumb both spake and saw.
Matthew 12:22

...a great multitude of people ... came to hear him, and to be healed of their diseases; And they that were vexed with unclean spirits: and they were healed.
Luke 6:17-18

...there met him ten men that were lepers, which stood afar off ... And it came to pass, that, as they went, they were cleansed.
Luke 17:12,14 (NKJV)

...he ... spake unto them of the kingdom of God, and healed them that had need of healing.
Luke 9:11

And they brought unto him also infants, that he would touch them...
Luke 18:15

...he [Jesus] cried with a loud voice ... And he that was dead came forth,
John 11:43-44

Jesus also did many other things. If they were all written down, I suppose the whole world could not contain the books that would be written.
John 21:25 (NLT)

With another Passover on the horizon, Jesus couldn't help but remember the event that placed such unrivalled power into this Feast called Passover. He *remembered* eons of ages ago! He *remembered* eternity past! **He *remembered***

the slaying of a Lamb long before the foundations of the world were formed!

He *remembered* His passion yet to be demonstrated. He *remembered* His passion for a Bride yet to be created. He *remembered* the Meal He would institute in conjunction with His last earthly Passover Meal.

It was the Meal of *Remembrance*—a Meal called Communion.

Jesus *remembered* while in the village of Capernaum. (Capernaum was the place Jesus moved to after John the Baptist, his cousin, had been put into prison.) Capernaum means: Village of Comfort.[23] After John's arrest, Jesus' heart needed comfort.

> *When Jesus got word that John had been arrested, he returned to Galilee. He moved from his hometown, Nazareth, to the lakeside village Capernaum...*
> *Matthew 4:12-13 (MSG)*

In this Village of Comfort, Jesus was thinking about the Meal of Remembrance—an often-forgotten, yet highly effective, secret weapon in our spiritual arsenal. With Passover just ahead, Jesus began to disclose the mystery in this Meal.

---

23   Interlinear Concordance, *Blue Letter Bible*, iPhone ed., v. 2.54 (Blue Letter Bible, 2016).

Standing in a synagogue in Capernaum, Jesus spoke to the people. He started out easy enough...

> *Do not work for the food which perishes, but for the food which endures to eternal life, which the Son of Man will give to you...*
> *John 6:27 (AMP)*

His words resounded throughout the multitudes—and should echo in our souls today. Do we consume and strive for temporary food more than we do for eternal food? Does the everlasting, perpetual, enduring food of the spirit realm hold great value to us; or, is that which we can touch, feel, and see in the natural realm captivating all our attention? Do we comprehend the effectiveness and power of the natural, yet spiritual, Meal of Passover and Communion?

Burning love for the people permeated the soul of Jesus! *Passover was coming ...* **did they know what they would be consuming?**

Passionately, He continued His "Bread of Life" discourse. Assuming that Jesus spoke about the wilderness manna, they pleaded with Him. "Our fathers ate manna ... bread out of Heaven.[24] Lord, always give us this bread!"[25]

---

24   John 6:31 (NASB) "Our fathers ate the manna in the wilderness; as it is written, He gave them bread out of heaven to eat."

25   John 6:34 (NASB) "Then they said to Him, Lord, always give us this bread."

Jesus' answer shook them to the core. "**I** AM the Bread of Life! **I** AM the Bread that came down from Heaven."

> *...I am the bread of life: he that cometh to me shall never hunger; and he that believeth on me shall never thirst.*
> *John 6:35*

> *I am that bread of life.*
> *John 6:48*

> *I am the living bread which came down from heaven: if any man eat of this bread, he shall live for ever: and the bread that I will give is my flesh, which I will give for the life of the world.*
> *John 6:51*

Distress and disillusionment shook the crowds. Passion, anger, offense, shock, sadness, confusion—the emotions churned inside of them. Jesus' passionate words *incited agitation* or *ignited passion* in the heart and soul of every person who heard His words. His flesh—the Bread of Heaven. Offended, they could not comprehend that their passionate redemption would be purchased by His perfect blood and broken body.

Shocked and confused, the crowds were bewildered. What kind of man would dare to speak in such a way?

...if it be lawful to call him a man ... He was [the] Christ;"[26]
—Flavius Josephus

Their minds and hearts simply could not understand...

But Jesus didn't give an inch...
John 6:53 (MSG)

He was not finished speaking yet. As Passover drew near, His purpose and passion resounded throughout His very being so fervently that He just could not stay silent. They must know, they must be informed, they must realize ... He must tell them! **The mystery of Passover must become revelation!**

> *So Jesus said to them, "Truly, truly, I say to you, unless you eat the flesh of the Son of Man and drink His blood, you have no life in yourselves.*
>
> *He who eats My flesh and drinks My blood has eternal life, and I will raise him up on the last day.*
>
> *For My flesh is true food, and My blood is true drink.*

---

26   William Whiston, Taken from *Josephus The Complete Works,* by William Whiston, A.M., 1998. Nashville, TN: Thomas Nelson Publishers, pg. 576. Used by permission of Thomas Nelson. www.thomasnelson.com.

He who eats My flesh and drinks My blood abides in Me, and I in him.

As the living Father sent Me, and I live because of the Father, so he who eats Me, he also will live because of Me.

This is the bread which came down out of heaven; not as the fathers ate and died; he who eats this bread will live forever."
John 6:53-58 (NASB)

Jesus eagerly desired for them to know that **HE IS the PASSOVER! HE IS the powerful mystery of Passover and the powerful reality of Communion!**

But, even partial disclosure of that mystery was more than they could bear! Offended by the mysterious truth of the power contained in consuming the Lord, many turned away and "walked no more with Him."[27]

Knowing the turbulent confusion in His followers, He made this statement about His "Bread of Life" discourse:

…Every word I've spoken to you is a Spirit-word, and so it is life-making. But some of you are resisting, refusing to have any part in this.
John 6:63 (MSG)

---

27   John 6:66 "From that time many of his disciples went back, and walked no more with him."

...the words that I speak unto you, they are
spirit, and they are life.
John 6:63

As the crowds dissipated, Jesus turned to His disciples and asked,

"Are you also going to leave?"
John 6:67 (NLT)

But, they knew His words were words of life. In passionate resolve...

Peter replied, "Master, to whom would we go?
You have the words of real life, eternal life. We've
already committed ourselves, confident that you
are the Holy One of God."
John 6:68-69 (MSG)

From the beginning of Passover's institution as a Meal, the flesh and blood of the powerful Passover Lamb caused a distinct separation between those who were truly God's people and those who were not. The masses left in offense, the disciples drew near in love.

I will make a clear distinction between my
people and your people...
Exodus 8:23 (NLT)

Passover's corresponding Meal—Communion—also causes a distinction. It is a Meal that ignites or incites! It ignites passion, causing us to draw nearer to Him; *or*, it incites offense and indignation, causing us to turn away. His Body and His Blood will forever be the true dividing line of distinction.

My prayer is that you will never be offended at the mystery of Jesus contained in the eating and drinking of the Bread and the Wine. As you embrace the Communion/Passover Meal, the immortal life and grace of Jesus Christ will encircle and envelop you! This wondrously mystical[28] Meal will cause you to be distinctly separate from the world. This Meal transcends human understanding!

> *To whom God would make known what is the riches of the glory of this **mystery ... which is Christ in you...***
> *Colossians 1:27*

Christ *in* you! Consume Him! And as you do, you will be filled with the riches of His glory.

It is a mystery—how can one Meal fill us with all the glorious blessings of Heaven? It seems unfathomable to the human mind, but He proves His faithfulness over and over again as Heaven's power is unleashed and released when we partake of Him! He will fill your very being with Heaven's capacity.

---

28 "Mystical: transcending human understanding; inspiring a sense of spiritual mystery, awe, and fascination; concerned with the soul or the spirit, rather than with material things."
New Oxford American Dictionary, (2010), s.v. "mystical."

12. Eternal Passover Lamb

Now the feast of unleavened bread drew nigh,
which is called the Passover.
                    Luke 22:1 (NKJV)

Jesus steadfastly set His face toward Jerusalem! Passover, once again, was drawing near.

And the Jew's Passover was nigh at hand: and
many went out of the country up to Jerusalem
before the Passover...
                    John 11:55

Jesus was ready! This wouldn't be just another Passover; this would be *the* Passover—His last "earthly" one! And this year, He didn't walk there! He rode into Jerusalem on a donkey. (Jesus had made a significant choice of mount. In ancient times, if the king rode into a city on a horse, he came on a mission of war; but when a king rode in on a donkey, his mission was one of peace.)

Please note: The next time Jesus rides in, He will be mounted on a white horse!

And I saw heaven opened, and behold a white horse; and he that sat upon him was called Faithful and True, and in righteousness he doth judge and make war.

His eyes were as a flame of fire, and on his head were many crowns; and he had a name written, that no man knew, but he himself.

And he was clothed with a vesture dipped in blood: and his name is called The Word of God.

And the armies which were in heaven followed him upon white horses, clothed in fine linen, white and clean.

And out of his mouth goeth a sharp sword, that with it he should smite the nations: and he shall rule them with a rod of iron: and he treadeth the winepress of the fierceness and wrath of Almighty God.

And he hath on his vesture and on his thigh a name written, KING OF KINGS, AND LORD OF LORDS.
Revelation 19:11-16

However, this Passover season, Jesus rode in on a donkey. Not here to subjugate with military force, our Messiah had come to bring peace to the earth!

> Peace I leave with you, my peace I give unto you...
>
> John 14:27

> ...that in me ye might have peace.
>
> John 16:33

In fulfilment of Zechariah's prophetic declaration, Jesus signified that He *is*, indeed, a King; and, He *is* bringing salvation.

> Rejoice greatly, O daughter of Zion; shout, O daughter of Jerusalem: behold, **thy King** cometh unto thee: he is just, and **having salvation**; lowly, and riding upon an ass...
>
> Zechariah 9:9

Jesus rode into Jerusalem as massive crowds cheered and shouted. Soon He would be left in absolute abandonment, but for now they proclaimed His true and eternal title as they...

> Took branches of palm trees, and went forth to meet him, and cried, Hosanna: Blessed is the **King of Israel** that cometh in the name of the Lord.
>
> John 12:13

Years earlier, John the Baptist declared that Jesus was the long-awaited Messiah as he made the paradigm-shifting statement, "Behold the Lamb of God!"

> ...he saw Jesus coming to him and said, "Behold, the Lamb of God who takes away the sin of the world!
>
> *John 1:29 (NASB)*

But now, John the Baptist was imprisoned. John remembered the day that the Dove descended and remained on Jesus. This heavenly recognition signified that Jesus was the One Who would baptize with the Holy Ghost.

> And I myself did not know him, but the one who sent me to baptize with water told me, 'The man on whom you see the Spirit come down and remain is the one who will baptize with the Holy Spirit.'
>
> *John 1:33 (NIV)*

John clearly remembered the day that Heaven's voice echoed through the desert.

> And behold, a voice out of the heavens said, "This is My beloved Son, in whom I am well-pleased."
>
> *Matthew 3:17 (NASB)*

John certainly remembered declaring that Jesus was the Son of God.

And I saw, and bare record that this is the Son of God.
John 1:34

Yet, sitting in the darkness of prison, He just finally had to ask.

Summoning two of his disciples, John sent them to the Lord, saying, "Are You the Expected One, or do we look for someone else?"
Luke 7:19 (NASB)

Instead of directly answering John's question, Jesus instructed them to testify to John of the things they had seen and heard. Testimonies were plentiful; but Jesus specifically pointed out four miracles that all of Israel knew were signs of the Messiah.

Then Jesus answering said unto them, Go your way, and tell John what things ye have seen and heard; how that the blind see, the lame walk, the lepers are cleansed, the deaf hear, the dead are raised, to the poor the gospel is preached.
Luke 7:22

Four expected Messianic miracles were:

1. Healing a leper
2. Casting out a mute demon
3. Healing a man born blind
4. Raising someone from the dead after four days

When John received the news that these miracles had been performed, he was once again convinced that Jesus was the Messiah—and, most certainly, the Lamb of God!

Jesus, Son of God yet Son of Man, was the Lamb. It was the priest's duty to confirm the Passover Lamb and John belonged not just to the Levitical lineage, but even more explicitly, the Aaronic priesthood.

> *...there was a priest named Zacharias, of the division of Abijah; and he had a wife from the daughters of Aaron, and her name was Elizabeth.*
> *Luke 1:5 (NASB)*

John's father and mother were *both* blood descendants from Aaron's priesthood lineage. Therefore, John the Baptist had the right to confirm the "Lamb of God."

Lamb of God! King of kings! Messiah of the world! In the month of Nisan, the Lamb of God made His triumphal entry into Jerusalem, knowing that Calvary was ahead of Him. Masses cheered, and children giggled; excitement and anticipation permeated the atmosphere. Bethlehem's lambs were arriving in the city for the Passover Feast.

Passover ... what would be released?

13. Shadow to Image

...they made ready the Passover...
Matthew 26:19 (NKJV)

Jesus' disciples had heard John the Baptist declare that
Jesus was the *"Lamb of God Who takes away the sin of the
world,"* yet they did not grasp the reality of what John
said. Had they understood the revelation of this statement, they never would have debated as to whether those
born outside of the Jewish race could receive the salvation
of God.

> *But when Peter arrived back in Jerusalem, the
> Jewish believers criticized him... Then Peter
> told them exactly what had happened... When
> the others heard this, they stopped objecting and
> began praising God. They said, "We can see that
> God has also given the Gentiles the privilege of
> repenting of their sins and receiving eternal life."*
> *Acts 11:2,4,18 (NLT)*

In Egypt, one lamb wrought deliverance for
one household.

…In the tenth day of this month they shall take
to them every man a lamb…a lamb for an house:
Exodus 12:3

God's Lamb would extend redemption to the entirety of the "world."

This Passover was Jesus' last earthly Passover, His final week of earthly life. It was now that Jesus would take the "shadow" of an Old Testament ritual and turn it into the "very image" of New Testament reality.

The old system under the law of Moses was only
a shadow, a dim preview of the good things to
come, not the good things themselves…
Hebrews 10:1 (NLT)

For close to 1500 years, the Israelite nation had eaten of the Passover Lamb. As Jesus reached His last Passover on earth, He unveiled a sacred secret concealed from the beginning of time. He made known a…

…revelation of the mystery, which was kept
secret since the world began, But now is
made manifest…
Romans 16:25-26

Jesus' sacred secret was that **He *is* the Passover**.

*…this **is** my body…*
Matthew 26:26

**JESUS is our Mystery Feast
which contains all the power of Heaven.**

Not long ago, Jesus had declared that He *was* the Bread of Heaven.

> *I am that bread of life ... This is the bread which cometh down from heaven, that a man may eat thereof, and not die.*
> *John 6:48,50*

> *I am the living bread which came down from heaven: if any man eat of this bread, he shall live for ever...*
> *John 6:51a*

> *...and the bread that I will give is my flesh, which I will give for the life of the **world**.*
> *John 6:51b*

> *...Verily, verily, I say unto you, Except ye eat the flesh of the Son of man, and drink his blood, ye have no life in you.*
> *John 6:53*

> *Whoso eateth my flesh, and drinketh my blood, hath eternal life...*
> *John 6:54*

This caused many of His followers to turn away. But now, Jesus asked His disciples to **eat** of that Bread...

*...and they prepared the Passover ... And as they were eating, Jesus took bread ... said, Take, eat; **this is my body**. And he took the cup ... saying ... **this is my blood** of the new testament...*
Matthew 26:19,26-28 (NKJV)

Once again, Passover's miracle of distinction took place as the dividing line of His Body and Blood was laid out. Jesus' words ignited passion in the hearts of His disciples, but quickly incited agitation in the heart of the one who would betray Him. In true Passover form, distinction was made. Judas turned and walked away.

I will make a clear distinction between my people and your people...
Exodus 8:23 (NLT)

Jesus, the eternal Lamb, *is* the reality of the shadow. The veil was about to be torn; New Testament truth was about to be unveiled.

During His final earthly Passover, and His final moments with His disciples (from here on, Jesus walks out His purpose for coming to earth alone), Jesus wants them to know: *He* is the world's redemption, *He* is the world's salvation, and *He* is the One Who would secure man's emancipation.

...I came ... to save the world.
John 12:47

*Jesus **is** Passover ... the Meal of Release.*

14. Communion Instituted

…Christ our Passover…
1 Corinthians 5:7

A sacred secret about the powerful feast of Christ—Communion—had been hidden in the form of the powerful Passover Meal all these many generations!

And as they were eating, Jesus took bread, and blessed it, and brake it … And he took the cup, and gave thanks, and gave it to them…
Matthew 26:26-27

Jesus, knowing the road ahead of Him, still "gave thanks" for the Passover Bread and Cup.

It was the symbol of His suffering and death. Yet, He spoke a blessing over it and gave thanks for it. For those who give thanks in all things have the power to turn curses into blessings … and sorrows into joy … the power of the eucharistia … to live a life of blessing.
—Jonathan Cahn

He knew the power of this Passover meal, and He knew what would come "on the morrow."

> *The Lord of hosts will prepare a lavish banquet for all peoples on this mountain ... He will swallow up death for all time.*
> *Isaiah 25:6,8 (NASB)*

"On the morrow" it would be Him against hell. "On the morrow" He would single-handedly wage a cosmic war with death. "On the morrow" His Father would turn away, leaving Him *alone*. Separation from His Father—oh, the torture and anguish! That was greater than any hell He would face, any torture He would endure, and any death He would die. No wonder He eagerly desired to partake of this Passover. He was going to need every bit of Heaven's powerful capacity for the job ahead of Him—tomorrow!

Gave thanks is the Greek word [eucharisteo]. Holding the Passover Bread and Cup, Jesus did *eucharisteo;* and Eucharist, or Holy Communion, was instituted.

> *The cup of blessing which we bless, is it not the communion of the blood of Christ? The bread which we break, is it not the communion of the body of Christ?*
> *1 Corinthians 10:16*

Countless lambs had been sacrificed year after year after year, after century, after millennia. But, Heaven's Lamb was so perfect and so flawless that never again would another earthly lamb need to be slain to take away sin, or sin-consciousness. Those lambs were just a "shadow of good things to come," but the Lamb Jesus Christ was the "very image."

> For the law having a **shadow** of good things to come, and not the **very image** of the things, can never with those sacrifices which they offered year by year continually make the comers thereunto perfect.
> *Hebrews 10:1*

> The sacrifices under that system were repeated again and again, year after year, but they were never able to provide perfect cleansing for those who came to worship.
> *Hebrews 10:1 (NLT)*

Even while knowing the destiny of a Passover lamb was imminent death, the Holy Lamb of God "gave thanks." With complete humility, **Jesus reached for the Bread, broke it and *gave thanks for His broken body.*** By one offering, He would perfect and release us forever—release us from sin, shame, sickness, and lack, release us from bondage and set us free from the law of sin and death. Jesus—the Eternal, Holy, Sublime Lamb of Heaven—incomparable, unexcelled, unsurpassed, unequalled, unrivalled. Our Passover, our Meal!

In His final moments of intimate, personal "communion" with His disciples, Jesus shared the most important meal with them. Here Jesus didn't just eat the Meal, He became the Meal.

He became Passover—the Meal of Release.
He became Communion—the Meal of Remembrance!

> *And he took bread, gave thanks and broke it, and gave it to them, saying, "This **is** my body given for you; do this in remembrance of me."*
> *Luke 22:19 (NIV)*

Jesus declared to His disciples, "Do this in remembrance of me!" *Remembrance* is the Greek word [anamnesis].

Anamnesis is a key concept: ***in worship the faithful recall God's saving deeds.***[29]

The faithful … those whose hearts were *ignited* by His words and His meal. The faithful … would they finally understand? Had He said enough? Had He revealed enough? Would they finally realize, when they saw Him hanging on the cross, that He was the Passover Lamb slain for the redemption of the world? Would they realize the *life* and *release* contained and demonstrated so many, many times through the consuming of Passover was, in actuality, Heaven's very Life-force contained in Jesus Christ?

---

*...his divine power hath given unto us all things
that pertain unto life...*
2 Peter 1:3

In him was life...
John 1:4

Jesus said ... I am the resurrection, and the life...
John 11:25

Would they *remember* that they were eating the very
Bread of Life? Would they *remember* that it was His
Body and Blood? Would they *remember* to partake of
Communion? And to partake of it—often? Would His
Church be faithful?

Communion—in remembrance of our passionate
Passover Lamb! **Every time the faithful partake of it, *the
faithful recall God's saving deeds.***

Behold, the Lamb of God! Jesus Christ—the
unequalled, unrivalled capacity of Heaven contained in
this one earthly meal. The mystery had been revealed.
Jesus Christ is our Passover! *Jesus Christ* is our Meal!
Communion, our lavish banquet, was prepared.

*Communion ... a Meal made in Heaven ... the Meal
of Release!*

15. Release of Power for Destiny

Forsaken, abandoned, betrayed, and denied, no one stood with Jesus: not one adoring worshipper, not one healed individual, not one close friend... The One Who had drawn so many crowds stood completely alone, about to be examined and inspected by ruling authorities.

The band of men that arrested Jesus led him away to be examined by Annas, the High Priest. Annas then took Jesus to his son-in-law, Caiaphas. Caiaphas, also High Priest, had earlier given advice to the Jews while plotting to kill Jesus. His cruel counsel contained all the bitter venom of his hatred and jealousy towards Jesus, yet it was a prophetic statement that would ring throughout the corridors of time and eternity.

> ...it would be good for one man to die on behalf of the people.
> John 18:14 (CJB)

The elders, the council, and now the High Priests (all who so hated Jesus) searched for flaws. But, Jesus—fully God, yet fully man—was perfect in all His ways.

81

> *And the chief priests and all the council sought for witness against Jesus to put him to death; and **found none**.*
> *Mark 14:55*

No cause for death—He was perfect!

Those desiring His death hired false witnesses so that Jesus could, and would, be condemned by the Sanhedrin—the supreme judicial and administrative council of the Jews. Humiliation and torture began as they spit on Him, covered His face to beat Him with their fists, mocked, and struck Him out of sheer abhorrence and animosity.[30] Fulfilling Isaiah's Messianic prophecy, He was able to say,

> *...I was not disobedient nor did I turn back. I gave My back to those who strike Me, and My cheeks to those who pluck out the beard; I did not cover My face from humiliation and spitting.*
> *Isaiah 50:6 (NASB)*

> *...So His appearance was marred more than any man...*
> *Isaiah 52:14 (NASB)*

The Jewish leaders bound Jesus and delivered Him to Pilate. Jealously hating His divine influence and fame, they now dragged Him before one who could pronounce legal

---

30   Mark 14:64-65 (NIV) "...They all condemned him as worthy of death. Then some began to spit at him; they blindfolded him, struck him with their fists, and said, Prophesy! And the guards took him and beat him."

judgment. Jesus stood before Pontius Pilate, the procurator. (A procurator is an agent who represents others in a court of law in countries retaining Roman civil law.) The hateful mob clamored for His execution.

> *And though they found no ground for putting Him to death, they asked Pilate that He be executed.*
> *Acts 13:28 (NASB)*

Pilate began the examination, "Do you hear that they witness against you? Have you heard how many things they accuse you of?"

Like a lamb led to slaughter, Jesus remained silent. Only one question would get a response out of this Perfect One. It was a question of legality, one regarding *His Father's business.*

"Are you the King of the Jews?"

Pulsating with Pilate's question, Jesus couldn't help but *remember*... He *remembered* yesterday's enormous emotional stress as mankind's eternal life rested on His shoulders. He *remembered* the agonized thoughts of physical torture He would have to endure to redeem mankind. Yet His agony in the Garden was not about pain, but about forsakenness. His anguished plea pierced the skies,

"Father, save me from this hour!"[31] Yet, in perfect and submissive obedience, His response to His Father (and to Himself) was, **"For this cause I came..."**[32]

He also *remembered* yesterday's glorious moment when His Father's audible voice answered His cry.[33] Some people thought it thundered, others thought an angel spoke.[34] That voice He loved so dearly filled Him with increased resolve. It all happened just yesterday. Yesterday! But ... this was *tomorrow*.

He had partaken of Passover; and, tomorrow had arrived. With the strength, force, and tenacity of One filled with the unrivalled power of Passover, Jesus responded. Filled with Heaven's capacity, from the deepest depths of His being He cried—

"This is what I was born for, this is why I am here!"[35]

---

31   John 12:27 (NASB) "Now is my soul troubled; and what shall I say? Father, save me from this hour..."

32   John 12:27 (NASB) "...but for this cause came I unto this hour."

33   John 12: 28 "Father, glorify thy name. Then came there a voice from heaven, *saying*, I have both glorified *it*, and will glorify *it* again."

34   John 12:29 "The people therefore, that stood by, and heard it, said that it thundered: others said, An angel spake to him."

35   John 18:37 "Pilate therefore said unto him, Art thou a king then? Jesus answered, Thou sayest that I am a king. To this end was I born, and for this cause came I into the world..."

16. Faultless

Heaven's power filled Jesus' words! Pilate was shaken— and certain. Rendering his judicial judgment, Pilate the procurator, made a legal statement. **"... I find in him no fault at all."**[36]

No cause for death—He was faultless.

Enraged, the mob fiercely insisted that Jesus' claim of being the Son of God was responsible for stirring up all people in Jewry, from Galilee to Jerusalem.[37] Frightened by the claim of Christ, Pilate wondered where Jesus was from—Heaven or Galilee? "Is this man a Galilean?" Pilate questioned. Galilee's jurisdiction belonged to Herod Antipas; so, much to Herod's delight, Pilate sent Jesus to him. Herod had heard many things about Jesus and secretly hoped to see Him perform a miracle.

---

36   John 18:38 "Pilate saith unto him, What is truth? And when he had said this, he went out again unto the Jews, and saith unto them, I find in him no fault at all."

37   Luke 23:5 "And they were the more fierce, saying, He stirreth up the people, teaching throughout all Jewry, beginning from Galilee to this place."

But, Herod's many questions could not solicit a response from the silent Lamb. Not one word of rebuttal did Jesus give in self-defence; not one miracle did Herod see Him perform. Irritated and annoyed, Herod and his soldiers humiliated and mocked Jesus, then sent Him back to Pilate.

The Holy Lamb of Heaven was confirmed by John the Baptist—*Behold the Lamb of God.*

The Holy Lamb of Heaven was inspected by chief priests and the Sanhedrin, who found only a flawless record—*perfection.*

The Holy Lamb of Heaven was examined by judicial court, which discovered only an unblemished account—*faultless.*

Inspected in Jerusalem, our Passover Lamb was declared perfect and faultless. He was here on His Father's business—God was about to redeem mankind. This is what He was born for! This is why He had come! The One "whose shoe's latchet"[38] John the Baptist was not worthy to unloose had taken off His shoes. The sandals had come off and were given in perfect submission to His Father. There was about to be a **redeeming of property** and the **acquiring of a Bride.**

---

38   John 1:27 "He it is, who coming after me is preferred before me, whose shoe's latchet I am not worthy to unloose."

➤ <u>Redemption of Property</u>: The Prince of this World would be displaced by the Prince of Peace. The kingdoms of this world were about to become the kingdoms of our Lord.

> *…the government shall be upon his shoulder: and his name shall be called … The Prince of Peace. Of the increase of his government and peace there shall be no end…*
> *Isaiah 9:6-7*

> *…now shall the prince of this world be cast out.*
> *John 12:31*

➤ <u>Acquisition of a Bride</u>: Man's redemption was about to be purchased. Jesus—God's Son—was about to acquire a Bride!

> *Who gave himself for us to redeem us from all wickedness and to purify for himself a people that are his very own…*
> *Titus 2:14 (NIV)*

> *…Come hither, I will shew thee the bride, the Lamb's wife.*
> *Revelation 21:9*

Heaven's Passover was about to take place on earth!

17. The Unwritten Rule

As Pilate stood before the angry mob and their silent victim, He knew there was a custom that came into effect at Passover.

> But ye have a **custom**, that I should release unto you one at the Passover...
> *John 18:39*

Remember: **a custom is an unwritten rule**! And, in law, a custom has the force of right.

Even as a Roman, Pilate was aware of the unwritten, yet very obvious, principle connected with Passover. This principle or unwritten rule is: **Passover generates release**. Passover causes the release of a prisoner.

> For **of necessity** he must release one unto them at the feast.
> *Luke 23:17*

Passover was a day for pardoning prisoners! Israel's governing body had many prisoners, prisoners who knew that a release would be granted to one of them during the Passover. Those most innocent hoped against hope for *release*. Those who had committed the worst of crimes knew that they had absolutely no chance of pardon on the day of this most amazing, mysterious, release-generating Feast.

Greatly impacted by a troubling dream, Pilate's wife sent an urgent message to her husband. "Have nothing to do with that innocent man!"[39] Shaking and trembling, Pilate desperately wanted to release Jesus.[40] He knew Jesus was innocent. Every person in Jerusalem knew. Pilate wanted nothing to do with putting such a Man to death. The more Pilate appealed for release, the more enraged and infuriated the priestly authorities became. Pandemonium was ruling.

Convinced Jesus was innocent, Pilate had one more plan. He would pick the worst, most revolting prisoner he had—Barabbas, the murderer—then he would make the crowd choose between the release of Barabbas or Jesus. Surely no one would want the violent, revolutionist murderer back on the streets. Murderer or healer? The answer seemed obvious.

Yet, without a moment's hesitation, the religious leaders started chanting, "Barabbas! Barabbas! Barabbas!"

---

39   Matthew 27:19 "While Pilate was sitting on the judge's seat, his wife sent him this message: Don't have anything to do with that innocent man, for I have suffered a great deal today in a dream because of him."

40   Luke 23:20 (NIV) "Wanting to release Jesus, Pilate appealed to them again."

In disbelief, Pilate shuddered as they demanded the innocent be put to death and the guilty be set free! Crumbling
from fatigue and stress, Pilate would do anything to have
these people leave.

"What is it you want?" he asked the screaming mob.

"Crucify him!" Uncontrollable, they screamed out the
most horrible, torturous, agonizing death they knew of.

> *And Pilate gave sentence that it should be as*
> *they required.*
> *Luke 23:24*

> *And he **released** the man they were asking for*
> *who had been thrown into prison for insur-*
> *rection and murder, but he delivered Jesus to*
> *their will.*
> *Luke 23:25 (NASB)*

A last-minute exchange was made! In disbelief and
shock, Barabbas came out of prison—pardoned! He
wanted to see the Man Who would be so horrid as to
cause a murderer's release. What could this Man have
done? The notorious prisoner eagerly scanned the crowd
for a worst-of-the-worst, heinous prisoner who had just
received his death sentence—execution on the stake, a
gruesome death penalty where every step of the execution
process was designed to increase the victim's humiliation
and intensify the victim's pain. Barabbas' gaze met eyes so

full of love that his entire guilt-ridden, murderous past was completely shattered forever. The unfeigned love emanating from Jesus enveloped the pardoned prisoner. This Man was Barabbas' substitute. Confused, Barabbas knew an exchange had been made! Many thoughts ran through his mind...

Jesus received: bondage for my release,
penalty for my wrongs,
judgment for my acquittal.

Jesus gave: His mercy for my ruthlessness,
His righteousness for my sinfulness,
His life for my death sentence.

Certainly, they had made a mistake! This man had done nothing deserving of death.

Pilate, manipulated and controlled by the rioting mob before him, had one more *legal* statement yet to make. It was another prophetic statement that would resound throughout heaven for all of eternity. Pilate knew the truth! From his place of judicial authority, Pilate echoed Heaven's words that had been resonating inside of him since he set eyes on this Man. The Roman agent governing on earth declared the words resounding throughout Heaven...

"Behold, your King!"[41]

The trial concluded; scourging, mockery and persecution continued. Execution had been sentenced and the innocent had been condemned. A sinless, sickless, sacrificial Lamb was headed to the altar.

Jesus Christ, the Lamb of God, was about to be slain!

---

41   John 19:14 "And it was the preparation of the Passover, and about the sixth hour: and he saith unto the Jews, Behold your King!"

18. Heaven's Passover

Picking up the cross constructed for Barabbas, the Son of Commandment set His face like flint and headed toward Golgotha, the "Place of the Skull." He was still about His Father's business.

> ...*as the Father gave me* **commandment**, *even so I do.*
> *John 14:31 (NKJV)*

Staying alive was not His first priority—obedience was. Voluntarily, He put aside His own desires to fulfil the commandments of His Father, and Father had given Him another command.

> ...*I lay down my life, that I might take it again. No man taketh it from me, but I lay it down of myself. I have power to lay it down, and I have power to take it again.* **This commandment have I received of my Father.**
> *John 10:18*

He would lay His life down for the passion of His heart—the world!

...Jesus ... for the joy that was set before him
endured the cross, despising the shame...
Hebrews 12:2

The King of Glory! Accustomed to the adoration of angels, He was now despised and rejected. Accustomed to the casting of crowns from heavenly elders, He was now whipped and tortured by mankind. Once surrounded with the singing of creation, His senses were now filled with piercing shouts of hatred and jealousy. He was used to being a warrior;[42] but here He was a prisoner. He was used to being a King;[43] but here He was a humble servant.[44] Heaven's ruling Lion[45] came to be earth's sacrificial Lamb. **Assuredly, He would receive the reward for His suffering!**

As Jesus reached the appointed place of execution, Heaven and earth synchronized on this crucial day. At the "third hour"[46] of the Jewish day (9:00 am), the Son of Man was lifted up to hang on the cross, fulfilling His own words of His own death.

---

42   Exodus 15:3 "The LORD is a man of war: the LORD is his name."

43   Psalm 24:10 "Who is this King of glory? The Lord of hosts, he is the King of glory. Selah."

44   Matthew 20:28 "Even as the Son of man came not to be ministered unto, but to minister, and to give his life a ransom for many."

45   Revelation 5:5 "...Weep not: behold, the Lion of the tribe of Juda, the Root of David, hath prevailed..."

46   Mark 15:25 "And it was the third hour, and they crucified him."

*And I, if I be **lifted up from the earth**, will draw all men unto me.*
                                    John 12:32

All the earth was about to be redeemed by their King! In perfect accordance with Heaven's plan, a prophetic Messianic Psalm sung by Jesus' earthly forefather David was being lived out in astounding accuracy.

Psalm 22
To the chief Musician upon Aijeleth Shahar,
A Psalm of David.

They open wide their mouth at me,
As a ravening and a roaring lion.

I am poured out like water,
And all my bones are out of joint;
My heart is like wax;
It is melted within me.

My strength is dried up like a potsherd,
And my tongue cleaves to my jaws;
And You lay me in the dust of death.

For dogs have surrounded me;
A band of evildoers has encompassed me;
They pierced my hands and my feet.

I can count all my bones.
They look, they stare at me;

They divide my garments among them,
And for my clothing they cast lots.

But You, O Lord, be not far off…
Psalm 22:13-19 (NASB)

At the "sixth hour" (12:00 noon), blackness invaded the earth.[47] As eerie darkness struck the land, Jesus screamed the despairing cry of ultimate abandonment, "My God, My God, why…?"[48] Heartbroken, He had reached the utter depth of suffering.

"…God (His Father) is light, and in Him is no darkness at all" (1 John 1:5). His Father turned away, the "Light" left. It was Him against the "power of darkness."[49] Although it was only noon, darkness prevailed over the earth for three hours.[50] Blacker than the blackness of Egypt's midnight, the world's darkest hour came as the Firstborn Son of God was slain.

My strength is dried up like a potsherd, And my
tongue cleaves to my jaws; And You lay me in the
dust of death.
Psalm 22:15 (NASB)

A potsherd is a piece of splintered earthenware—a piece so small it is no longer usable. Jesus' strength had been

---

47   Matthew 27:45 "Now from the sixth hour there was darkness over all the land unto the ninth hour."

48   Matthew 27:46 "About the ninth hour Jesus cried out with a loud voice, saying, Eli, Eli, lama sabachthani? that is, My God, My God, why have You forsaken Me?"

49   Luke 22:53 "…this is your hour, and the power of darkness."

50   Luke 23:44 "And it was about the sixth hour, and there was a darkness over all the earth until the ninth hour."

beaten down into the smallest, slivered pieces just like a piece of fragmented pottery. His strength was completely depleted and no longer usable. His mouth and tongue were so dry, so swollen with thirst and fever, that He could hardly speak. He was brought to the dust of death.

> Dust: [aphar]: pulverized, ground to powder or dust.

Pulverized by death, strength utterly fragmented, tongue completely adhered to His jaw, Jesus knew there was something He *must* do.

There He hung with every sin—of all ages, all humanity, and all people—upon Him. Not just the world's sin, but *my* sin! Not just the world's sin, but *your* sin! Every curse, calamity, cancer… every sin, sore, indignation… every awful effect of disease and sin crushed down on His body. And, sin always leads to separation from the Father, *that* was the greatest torture of all. He must not retain these sins; the price was far too high. He needed the forgiveness of His Father because *He* now held *every* sin of *every* person who would ever live. He definitely needed Father's forgiveness.

> *For if ye forgive men their trespasses, your heavenly Father will also forgive you: But if ye forgive not men their trespasses, neither will your Father forgive your trespasses.*
> *Matthew 6:14-15*

Forgive?! He must! Jesus mustered up enough shards of His strength to unstick His swollen tongue and utter words of *release*.

> ***...Father, forgive them...***
> *Luke 23:34*

Forgiveness—a most powerful spiritual weapon!
Forgiveness—release for the offender and release for the victim!

Forgiveness releases offenders from their executed sin and onslaught! Forgiveness releases victims from their prison of torturous mental agony!

Forgiveness is release!
Release ... the unwritten rule of Passover.

In excruciating agony, the Son of God hung suspended between Heaven and earth for six gruelling hours. Precisely at the "ninth hour" (3:00 pm) as the evening sacrifice was made in the Temple, Heaven's Passover Lamb was sacrificed on the Mount. At the ninth hour, as the priest released a shofar blast declaring that the lamb sacrifice was completed, Jesus released an even more powerful cry...

"IT IS FINISHED!"

Jesus' cry of triumph pierced the universe. His Father's command was executed. Heaven's perfect blood was shed on the earth. Remission of sins had been purchased.[51]

With midnight comes a new beginning. The world's turning point had come. The Lamb of God was sacrificed. A new era was about to dawn. Earth quaked calling to attention the great salvation that had been accomplished. Rocks split in two, graves opened, dead resurrected, and people trembled![52] Those, who had so cruelly slaughtered Heaven's Lamb, were in great dread. The centurion and his soldiers now understood. "Truly this man *was* the Son of God!"[53] What had they done?

The chief priests responsible for His death were in the Temple as an unprecedented phenomenon occurred—the Temple veil was torn in two. Suddenly able to see into the Holy of Holies—the very place where God's Presence dwelt—they stood transfixed in fear. Only once a year could the High Priest enter behind that veil. They did not

---

51   Matthew 26:28 "For this is my blood of the new testament, which is shed for many for the remission of sins."

52   Matthew 27:51-53 "And, behold, the veil of the temple was rent in twain from the top to the bottom; and the earth did quake, and the rocks rent; And the graves were opened; and many bodies of the saints which slept arose, And came out of the graves after his resurrection, and went into the holy city, and appeared unto many."

53   Mark 15:39 "And when the centurion, which stood over against him, saw that he so cried out, and gave up the ghost he said, Truly this man was the Son of God."

dare enter at the wrong time or in the wrong way. Access to the place of God's divine Presence required much purifying and preparation; and even then, the priest entered with much trepidation and fear. Never before had anything like this happened. Horrified, they stood staring at the Holy Place. Were they about to die?

The barrier between God and man had been removed by Heaven's Lamb. The way into God's Presence had just been opened up, giving access to everyone.[54]

> *…Christ our passover is sacrificed for us:*
> *1 Corinthians 5:7*

That Passover Day on Mt. Moriah, Abraham's prophetic words of so many centuries ago were fulfilled. GOD, HIMSELF, WILL PROVIDE A LAMB! (Genesis 22:8). On that momentous, earth-shaking, pivotal Passover day, one Lamb—Jesus Christ, the Lamb of God—took away the sin of the world.[55]

Passover's power and unwritten *law of release* was set in motion yet again. **Earth was released, thrust into a Dispensation of Grace!**

Jesus had just consummated Heaven's Perfect Passover.

---

54   Hebrews 10:19-20 "Having therefore, brethren, boldness to enter into the holiest by the blood of Jesus, By a new and living way, which he hath consecrated for us, through the veil, that is to say, his flesh;"

55   Wendy Varga, *Sacred Secret* (Victoria, BC: FriesenPress, 2017), pg 38.

19. Death's Destruction

In a supreme act of love, Jesus descended into the night of death. As His sacred head bowed on earth, He raised it in war inside the deepest abyss of hell's dungeon.

Now that he ascended, what is it but that he also descended first into the lower parts of the earth?
Ephesians 4:9

Imagine hell's surprise, as the Submissive Prisoner became the Unrivalled Warrior! The hordes of hell waged war with Heaven's Perfect Lamb Who had looked so weak and defeated just moments prior. He had not made one move to save His life as they tortured and killed Him. Now, He showed up in their very midst as a Triumphing War General. On a mission of redemption, He had come to set the captives free. The war was short and decisive! In a public showdown between Heaven and hell, Jesus Christ defeated them down to the very last enemy.

The last enemy that shall be destroyed is death.
1 Corinthians 15:26

It was not possible for death to hold Jesus in the grave!

> *Whom God hath raised up, having **loosed** the*
> ***pains** of death: because it was **not possible** that*
> *he should be **holden** of it.*
> *Acts 2:24*

Loosed: [luo]: destroyed, dissolved.

Pain: [odin]: pain (which is physical).
  sorrow (which is mental).
  travail (work that involves hard physical labor over a long period of time).

Possible: [dunatos]: powerful or capable.

Holden: [krateo]: to use strength, seize, or retain.

Death was not *powerful or capable* enough to hold Him down. Death could not, and did not, have enough strength to *seize or retain* Jesus Christ in the grave. In a cataclysmic battle for souls, Jesus was *laboring* to bring sons into the Kingdom. In His death, He was birthing many who would be called the *children of God*.

> *He shall see of the travail of his soul, and shall*
> *be satisfied...*
> *Isaiah 53:11*

...I will receive you. I will be a Father to you, and you shall be my sons and daughters, says the Lord Almighty.
2 Corinthians 6:17-18 (NIV)

Behold, what manner of love the Father hath bestowed upon us, that we should be called the sons of God...
1 John 3:1

Jesus Christ *destroyed and dissolved* every pain of death. The wounds and sufferings of perfect obedience became His power—destroying disease and afflictions of our bodies, along with mental torment and ailments of our souls. He dissolved every shackle, chain, oppression and sin. Death's work was dramatically reversed.

It was the moment of dethronement for all satan's powers.

And having spoiled principalities and powers, he made a shew of them openly, triumphing over them in it.
Colossians 2:15

...now shall the prince of this world be cast out.
John 12:31

Heaven's King took on every demonic power. For hell, the spectacle was humiliating and debilitating. Stripped of every power and every weapon they had possessed, they stood before all the hosts of Heaven—**rendered entirely useless**.

Using the very weapon satan used against Him, Jesus destroyed both death and the one who had wielded this power for so long. Satan was destroyed by his own weapon. Just as David took the sword from Goliath to cut off his head, Jesus took death from satan and cut off satan's *head*—his *governing rule*. His rule of authority and power was over. The devil was destroyed.

> *...he [Jesus] also himself likewise took part of the same; that **through death** he might destroy [render entirely useless][56] ... the devil;*
> *Hebrews 2:14 (definition added)*

Through all the previous millennia, life had always been swallowed up *into* death. Life had never *come out* of death. Jesus was the "firstborn of the dead" (Colossians 1:18). He was the first One to be swallowed by death and master it—completely.

> *...he is ... the firstborn from the dead...*
> *Colossians 1:18*

Death was mastered; hell was captured! Jesus Christ now held the "keys" of this realm.

---

56   "Destroy: [*katargeo*]: to render entirely useless."
"Interlinear KJV with Strong's Greek & Hebrew Lexicon," *SwordSearcher*, iPhone ed., v. 3.4 (Brandon Staggs, 1999).

*I ... was dead; and, behold, I am alive for ever-
more, Amen; and **have the keys of hell and
of death**.*
Revelation 1:18

Through death—the overpowering of it—Jesus became
the ruling authority of all.

*...he is ... the firstborn from the dead: **that in
all things he might have the preeminence**.*
Colossians 1:18

Pre-eminence is the fact of surpassing all others. The
supremacy of His Kingship had been sealed!

*...All power is given unto me in heaven and
in earth.*
Matthew 28:18

The war was over! Having disarmed powers and
principalities, Jesus Christ was about to resurrect! The
Triumphing King was still a Son of Commandment and
His Father's command was that He had the power to take
His life back up again. Heralding Christ's triumph over
sin and death, the recesses of the earth quaked violently.
The Unequivocal Power of Heaven began His ascent. His
radical love was stronger than death! He was *not* dead, but
He was alive! All of hell knew, all of Heaven knew; now,
the earth was about to find out!

...he shewed himself alive after his passion by many infallible proofs, being seen of them forty days, and speaking of the things pertaining to the kingdom of God:
Acts 1:3

...for he appeared to them alive again the third day, as the divine prophets had foretold these and ten thousand other wonderful things concerning him; and the tribe of Christians, so named from him, are not extinct at this day.[57]
—Flavius Josephus

Jesus Christ, God's Son, was alive! Principalities disarmed, world ruler cast out, death's dominion demolished—and Kingdom dispensation delivered. Earth was emerging from its dark chaos.

Heaven's perfect blood had bathed the world!

---

57   William Whiston, Taken from *Josephus The Complete Works,* by William Whiston, A.M., 1998. Nashville, TN: Thomas Nelson Publishers, pg. 576. Used by permission of Thomas Nelson. www.thomasnelson.com.

20. Doorposts of Your Heart

APPLICATION: Just as the blood of Passover lambs flowed throughout the land of Egypt, so His blood flows throughout the earth. Although the Passover blood was shed corporately, it still needed to be applied personally. Every doorpost of every family needed the blood applied in order to receive the life-saving, power-producing effects of that blood. Just as every doorpost needed blood application, so too, does every heart. Jesus shed His blood for the world, but it still needs to be applied to each individual heart. *You* are responsible for applying the blood of the Passover Lamb to *your* heart. Jesus has released Heaven's blood on the earth; you must apply Heaven's blood to your life. Faith in Jesus Christ is the only way to salvation.

For by grace are ye saved through faith...
Ephesians 2:8

Faith believes! But, faith always requires a voice, and your voice is the hyssop that applies His blood to your life.

*For with the heart man believeth unto righteous-
ness; and with the mouth confession is made
unto salvation.*
Romans 10:10

Jesus declared that He was the way to the Father![58] Jesus
said that He is life and whoever believes in Him would
receive this life. After all, He is the Son of Commandment,
and He…

…was not disobedient…
Isaiah 50:5 (NASB)

His Father sent Him down to earth to save the world.

*For God so loved the world, that he gave his only
begotten Son, that whosoever believeth in him
should not perish, but have everlasting life. For
God sent not his Son into the world to condemn
the world; but that the world through him might
be saved.*
John 3:16-17

"That the world might be saved!" Friend, the world
consists of *you*! As He endured the suffering and agony,
He did it for the joy that was before Him, and … *you*
were that joy! He died with passion, and … *you* were that
passion! He did everything … for *you*! Because of the love
He had … for *you*!

---

58   John 14:6 "Jesus saith unto him, I am the way, the truth, and the life: no
man cometh unto the Father, but by me."

You are the reason He came. *You* are the one who captured His heart. As God looked through the ages of eternity, He saw ... *you*!

>*...He [God] loved us, and sent his Son to be the propitiation for our sins.*
>*1 John 4:10*

>*...Christ also hath loved us, and hath given himself for us an offering and a sacrifice...*
>*Ephesians 5:2*

In His great passion, He traded places with us just as He traded places with Barabbas, the prisoner. We, too, were prisoners held in the grip of sin.

>*...the Scriptures declare that we are all prisoners of sin, so we receive God's promise of freedom only by believing in Jesus Christ.*
>*Galatians 3:22 (NLT)*

Jesus—in His great passion—set us free from the prison of sin!

>*And through Him **everyone who believes is freed** from all things, from which you could not be freed through the law of Moses.*
>*Acts 13:39 (NASB)*

Jesus became man's substitute. The application of Jesus' blood brings us into justification. Justification—the act of our pardon. Jesus carried our sin so that we may carry His righteousness.

> ...*my righteous servant [Jesus] will* **justify** *many, and he will bear their iniquities.*
> *Isaiah 53:11 (NIV)*

> Justification: a forensic term, opposed to condemnation. As regards its nature, it is the judicial act of God, by which he *pardons* all the sins of those who believe in Christ ... and treats them as righteous in the eye of the law, i.e., as conformed to all its demands. ... *The law is not relaxed or set aside, but is declared to be fulfilled in the strictest sense*; and so **the person justified is declared to be entitled to all the advantages and rewards arising from perfect obedience to the law**. *Justification is not the forgiveness of a man without righteousness, but a declaration that he possesses a righteousness which perfectly and for ever satisfies the law, namely,* <u>*Christ's righteousness*</u>.[59]

Faith is the only way to apprehend the righteousness of Jesus Christ and release your debt of sin. Your heart must believe, and your mouth must speak!

Have you applied the blood of Heaven's Perfect Lamb to your heart and life? He is waiting for you to make Him

---

59   "Easton's Bible Dictionary," *SwordSearcher*, iPhone ed., v. 3.4 (Brandon Staggs, 1999).

your personal Passover Lamb! As you do, you become His child. You become His great delight. You become the reward of His suffering—and, for Him, that made it all worthwhile.

> *Yet it pleased the LORD to bruise him [Jesus]*
> *... when thou [YOU*] shalt make his soul an*
> *offering for sin, he shall see his seed [YOU*], ...*
> *He shall see of the travail of his soul [YOU*],*
> ***and shall be satisfied:***
> *Isaiah 53:10-11 [paraphrase*: author's]*

➢ Take a moment, right now, to apply Jesus' blood to your heart. With faith, declare, "**Jesus Christ—the One Who triumphed over death and hell—is Lord and King of my life!**" By faith, you have just become His reward. You have become the Child of God. You bring His soul great satisfaction. You have been forgiven. You have been pardoned. He now declares you justified—*entitled to all the advantages and rewards arising from perfect obedience.* You have been given the righteousness of Jesus Christ, the Son of Commandment! His perfect obedience, and the rewards of it, have now been relegated to you. Jesus delivered you from the power of satan and from the power of darkness! Welcome to the Kingdom!

> *He has rescued us from the domain of darkness and transferred us into the Kingdom of his dear Son.*
> *Colossians 1:13 (CJB)*

Christ, our Passover Lamb, has released you and I into His Kingdom and into His life. As you know the power of His death, may you also know the power of His Resurrection!

> *For if we have been planted together in the likeness of his death, we shall be also in the likeness of his resurrection:*
> *Romans 6:5*

21. Resurrection's First Mission

He is not here: for he is risen...
Matthew 28:6

The Sabbath after the crucifixion seemed to never end. There was little they could do and even less that they wanted to do. The traumatic setback of His death, was nearly more than His followers could handle. For three years, the eleven disciples and many others had dedicated their lives to following and learning from Jesus. Yesterday He died, today was Sabbath—and tomorrow? Tomorrow, who knew? What could tomorrow possibly hold? Certainly, no hope. They were stymied.

Their Messiah was to bring a Kingdom, but the Kingdom didn't arrive as they might have expected. Overcome by a sense of crushing defeat, each had their own plans for tomorrow. The women, who just yesterday had prepared spices for His body, knew they were headed for the tomb as soon as the restrictions of Sabbath were past.[60] Some were undecided; some were heading home.

On the morrow, as Mary, Mary Magdalene, Joanna, Salome, and other women[61] neared the tomb, they began to wonder how they would get into the tomb to anoint His beloved body. Who would roll the stone away from the sepulchre door? Perplexed, they reached the tomb and found the very huge stone rolled away. Who had moved it? Nervously, they entered the tomb. It was empty!

> *While they were perplexed about this, behold, two men suddenly stood near them in dazzling clothing; and as the women were terrified and bowed their faces to the ground, the men said to them, "Why do you seek the living One among the dead? He is not here, but He has risen...*
> *Luke 24:4-6 (NASB)*

Fear and joy filled the women as they ran to tell the others. But Mary Magdalene could not leave. She stood weeping. Where was her Lord? Where was the One Who had loved her so truly? As she turned, she saw another

---

60   Luke 23:56 "And they returned and prepared spices and ointments; and rested the sabbath day according to the commandment."

61   Mark 16:1 "And when the sabbath was past, Mary Magdalene, and Mary the mother of James, and Salome, had bought sweet spices, that they might come and anoint him."
Luke 24:10 "It was Mary Magdalene, and Joanna, and Mary the mother of James, and other women that were with them, which told these things unto the apostles."

Man. Thinking He was the gardener, she cried, "Where have you taken my Lord, tell me and I will take Him away?"

"Mary!"

The passion she felt every time He spoke her name filled her being. She knew! She knew! It was Him! "Rabboni!" She reached out to touch the One her soul did love.

"Touch me not;" Jesus said to Mary, "for I am not yet ascended to my Father: but go to my brethren, and say unto them, I ascend unto my Father, and your Father; and to my God, and your God." (John 20:17).

She would *obey*, for she *loved* him. She must tell the disciples.

The words rushed out of the women's mouths fast and furiously. Could it be? Could it possibly be? Unable to comprehend the magnificent message of resurrection, the group of disciples just looked at the women, wondering if they had lost their minds.

> *...these words appeared to them as nonsense,*
> *and they would not believe them.*
> *Luke 24:11 (NASB)*

But the women kept insisting that Jesus was not in the grave, so Peter and John ran to the sepulchre. They, too, saw the stone rolled away; they saw the empty linen clothes lying flat as though His sacred body had simply vanished out of them. Finally, Peter and John believed the women's report about the empty grave;[62] but, they did not see the angels, or their Lord. What had happened?! Unable to fathom the events that had occurred over the last few days during this historic Passover Feast, they turned around and headed home. Their journey back was much slower and contemplative.

> For as yet they knew not the scripture, that he
> must rise again from the dead.
> John 20:9 (NASB)

Jesus had spoken so many things to them during the last three years. They had seen more in a few short years than most would see in a lifetime. They had endured so many paradigm shifts and mindset changes that they weren't quite sure what to believe now. Jesus had said that *He* was the Bread of Life. Jesus had said that the Passover Meal was *His* Body and *His* Blood. He said that the Kingdom of Heaven was "at hand." And, yes, He had spoken of His death and told them of a resurrection—but they just couldn't comprehend it. All they could say was *the tomb was empty*. Where was their Lord? They just did not know.

---

62   John 20:6-8 "Then cometh Simon Peter following him, and went into the sepulchre, and seeth the linen clothes lie, And the napkin, that was about his head, not lying with the linen clothes, but wrapped together in a place by itself. Then went in also that other disciple, which came first to the sepulchre, and he saw, and believed."

*And, behold, two of them went **that same day**
to a village called Emmaus...*
Luke 24:13

Cleopas and another disciple who had been with the group dejectedly left the apostles and those who had been with Jesus. They headed back home. What else were they to do? With about a seven-mile journey from Jerusalem to Emmaus, they had plenty of time to reminisce. *Jesus, what a mighty Prophet—mighty in word and mighty in deed. Had Jesus' mission entirely failed?!*

They had been sure that He was the long-awaited Messiah. They had hoped He would be the One to redeem Israel, but their every belief died as they witnessed the crucifixion. Their hope had been buried in a tomb. That had all happened three long days ago. And just this morning, the women saw visions of angels and an empty tomb.[63] Mary Magdalene insisted that she saw Jesus (but she didn't touch Him). Simon Peter and John also saw an empty tomb, but Jesus was nowhere to be found. So, what else were they to do? They couldn't sit in Jerusalem forever.

As Cleopas and his companion walked towards home, the crestfallen travellers were joined by the risen Christ. Jesus entered into conversation with them, listening emphatically as they poured out their doubts and pain of

---

63   Luke 24:23 "And when they found not his body, they came, saying, that they had also seen a vision of angels, which said that he was alive."

the past few days. Assuming He must be the only one in Jerusalem who did not hear of the dreadful events, they talked on. Although they had been His followers, they could not recognize Him. As they walked, Jesus began to weave the past days' events into the Scriptures. Step by step, Jesus unveiled Himself—the Mystery of Passover's Feast.

Interestingly, Jesus began His discourse with Moses—the era when Passover was first instituted. His expounding of the Scriptures continued right up until the recent crucifixion of the true Passover Lamb, showing them that every prophecy given of the Christ was fulfilled.[64] Jesus had fulfilled *all* things written about Him in:

1. The law of Moses,
2. The prophets,
3. The Psalms.

They still did not recognize Him, but their wounded hearts slowly ignited with fresh fire as He gave revelation after revelation of Himself—the Passover Lamb slain just three days before.

The three travellers arrived in Emmaus. When Jesus acted as though he would travel farther, Cleopas insisted

---

64   Luke 24:44 "And he said unto them, These are the words which I spake unto you, while I was yet with you, that all things must be fulfilled, which were written in the law of Moses, and in the prophets, and in the psalms, concerning me."

that Jesus should remain with them since the day was nearly over.

As they fed their still unknown Visitor some supper, Jesus reached for the bread. He just couldn't help it. Bread was His favorite meal! Just a few days ago, He had eagerly anticipated sharing it with His closest friends. Bread, it was part of the Meal of His Passion! Bread and Wine! He *remembered* the evening before His death … three days ago…

> …*as they were eating, Jesus took bread, and blessed it, and brake it, and gave it to the disciples…*
> *Matthew 26:26*

Jesus wondered! *Would they remember? Would they remember to partake of Him? Would they remember to consume the Bread and the Wine? Would they remember that HE was the Bread of Life and their Cup of Blessing?*

Would they remember this Cup was the New Testament in His blood? Did they even realize that just three days ago, as the Temple veil was torn, they had stepped into a New Testament era—a dispensation of grace? Would they remember to partake often? Would they? Did they? Will they? …

Here He was, on His resurrection day, with Bread before Him yet again. Desire overtook Him! He reached for the Bread and served His hosts.

...he took bread, and blessed it, and brake, and gave to them.

Luke 24:30

As they ate the Bread that Jesus served, their eyes were opened, and they knew Him.[65] Followers of Jesus had walked and talked with the Resurrected Christ all day, and they didn't even know it! But, as they ate, they received full revelation of Who they were with. The moment of recognition came in context with a Meal—the *Breaking of Bread.*[66]

When we break the Bread of Communion, the *unwritten rule* of release is *always* put into effect. Communion causes a **release** of revelation and a **release** of greater intimacy with our Great Redeemer and the Lover of our souls. In Communion, we reach the very heart of God. Communion—the eating of the Body and Blood of our Passover Lamb—will cause us to see Jesus in the reality and fullness of Who He really is!

Oh, it was the meal that He had so eagerly and intensely waited for. Communion with His disciples, that was what He loved. Giving them of Himself, that was His Passion. Sharing His intimate thoughts and feelings with them,

---

65   Luke 24:30-31 "And it came to pass, as he sat at meat with them, he took bread, and blessed it, and brake, and gave to them. And their eyes were opened, and they knew him; and he vanished out of their sight."

66   Luke 24:35 (NASB) "They began to relate their experiences on the road and how He was recognized by them in the breaking of the bread."

that was His yearning. How eagerly He desired to share Communion with His friends again! He gave the Bread. They took and ate—yet, He could not, He must not!

He *will not* again—**until** He is with us (all of us) in His Father's Kingdom. Jesus passionately watched as they ate of His Bread, then He…

> …*vanished out of their sight.*
> *Luke 24:31*

Significantly, (while with some of His disciples), the *last act Jesus performed before His death* and the *first act He performed after His resurrection* was the *Breaking of Bread.* On both sides of the Cross, Jesus served a passionately powerful Meal.

On both sides of the Cross, Jesus *broke bread.*

The Emmaus-bound travellers were now fully convinced that Jesus was alive. His profound wisdom, His intense passion, His manner of speaking, and their burning hearts should have been enough to prove it. But, it was the *Breaking of Bread* that opened their minds and their hearts to a jubilant reality—their Redeemer, the Redeemer of the world, was certainly alive!

Although it was now evening, they immediately rushed back to Jerusalem to find their friends. They had a message to relay:

"The Lord is risen indeed!"[67]

As Cleopas and his companion shared the day's extraordinary events with the eleven disciples, Jesus appeared to them for the second time that day.[68] Shocked and terrified, the astonished disciples shrunk back from the One they loved. "Why are you troubled? Why do thoughts arise in your hearts? Behold … it is I!" (Luke 24:38-39).

Joy and wonder overtook the group!

Their Passover Lamb was truly alive!
Their Communion Meal was in their midst.

Once more with his disciples, this time Jesus asked for fish![69] He had things to tell them, so He must stay a while.

---

67   Luke 24:33-35 "And they rose up the same hour, and returned to Jerusalem, and found the eleven gathered together, and them that were with them, Saying, The Lord is risen indeed, and hath appeared to Simon. And they told what things were done in the way, and how he was known of them in breaking of bread."

68   Luke 24:36 "And as they thus spake, Jesus himself stood in the midst of them, and saith unto them, Peace be unto you."

69   Luke 24:41-43 "And while they yet believed not for joy, and wondered, he said unto them, Have ye here any meat? And they gave him a piece of a broiled fish, and of an honeycomb. And he took it, and did eat before them."

Again, starting with Moses, Jesus showed them how Christ—their Passover Lamb—was to suffer, die, and resurrect from the grave after three days. Today was that third day—*every prophetic sign of the Messiah was fulfilled.*

> *...Christ, our Passover Lamb, has been sacrificed for us.*
> *1 Corinthians 5:7*

22. Release from Prison

*...intending **after the Passover** to bring him...*
Acts 12:4 (NASB)

With Jesus Christ now ascended to His Father, the disciples carried on His work. Filled and empowered by the Holy Spirit, the Apostle Peter, denier of the Lord, now fearlessly proclaimed and demonstrated the Kingdom's power! After all, Peter had learned from the true Passover Lamb! But Herod the King was on a ruthless rampage.

> *About that time King Herod laid hands on some from the church to harm them. He had James, the brother of John, executed with a sword. When he saw that this pleased the Jews, he proceeded to arrest Peter too. (This took place during the feast of Unleavened Bread.) When he had seized him, he put him in prison, handing him over to four squads of soldiers to guard him. Herod planned to bring him out for public trial **after the Passover.***
> *Acts 12:1-4 (NET)*

Determined to destroy Christ's followers, Herod caused the church to suffer greatly. With James already executed by a sword, Herod would wait until *after* the Passover to have Peter executed.

> *...Herod's intention was to deliver Peter to the*
> *Jews for execution after the Passover.*
> Acts 12:4 (TLB)

Did Herod not know or understand Passover's unwritten rule? Did he not know that **Passover generates release**?

Darkness fell as night descended! *Tomorrow* had come. With the Feast now over, an incredible release of Heaven's power was about to be unleashed once more.

> ***The very night*** *before Herod was to bring him*
> *forward, Peter was sleeping between two sol-*
> *diers, bound with two chains, and sentries were*
> *in front of the door guarding the prison.*
> Acts 12:6 (AMP)

Before morning could even dawn, Passover's release was generated. *Release from bondage* and *de-activation of death* occurred yet once more! As the Church ascended in worship, Heaven's angel descended in war! This angel was on an assignment of release.

> *On the very night when Herod was about to*
> *bring him forward, Peter was sleeping between*
> *two soldiers, bound with two chains, and guards*

*in front of the door were watching over the
prison. And behold, an angel of the Lord suddenly appeared and a light shone in the cell; and
he struck Peter's side and woke him up, saying,
"Get up quickly." And his chains fell off his
hands. And the angel said to him, "Gird yourself
and put on your sandals." And he did so...*
Acts 12:6-9 (NASB)

Peter had taken his sandals off. Did he know? Did Peter
understand the signal of exchange and redemption; did he
understand the legal application put into effect through
the removal of sandals? Another exchange was about to
take place!

*And he said to him, "Wrap your cloak around
you and follow me." And he went out and
continued to follow, and he did not know that
what was being done by the angel was real, but
thought he was seeing a vision. When they had
passed the first and second guard, they came
to the iron gate that leads into the city, which
opened for them by itself; and they went out
and went along one street, and immediately the
angel departed from him. When Peter came to
himself, he said, "Now I know for sure that the
Lord has sent forth His angel and rescued me
from the hand of Herod and from all that the
Jewish people were expecting."*
Acts 12:6-11 (NASB)

With Passover finished and morning's arrival, Herod demanded Peter be brought out of prison for trial. The King was completely unaware that the unwritten rule of Passover had already been put into effect. Peter's release was secured, yet prison officials were carefully guarding Peter's empty prison cell just as Roman soldiers had carefully guarded Jesus' empty tomb. Chaos and commotion ruled.

> *At dawn there was a great commotion among the soldiers about what had happened to Peter. Herod Agrippa ordered a thorough search for him...*
> *Acts 12:18-19 (TLB)*

Although the resurrected Christ had ascended to the Father, **the principle of release was still in effect**. The same principle applied at the very first Passover in Egypt was applied again, some 1500 years later.

The principle:
➜ destruction of the enemy but deliverance of His children...

> *...He smote the Egyptians, but spared our homes...*
> *Exodus 12:27 (NASB)*

Peter was spared ... and ... his captors were executed.

When Herod had searched for him and had not found him, he examined the guards and ordered that they be led away to execution...
Acts 12:19 (NASB)

Another exchange had been made! Peter had made Christ his Lord. Lordship denotes ownership! Peter *belonged* to Christ; and, Christ's Passover power was promulgated in Peter's life. Promulgate means: put a law or decree into effect by official proclamation. Passover's spiritual law of release was promulgated, superseding Herod's earthly law. Peter was spared from execution!

Heaven's ability to supersede all earthly governmental power was *put into effect*.

At the Passover of Christ's crucifixion, Barabbas (a notorious sinner) was released from prison and execution. At a Passover after Christ's ascension, Peter (a dedicated disciple) was released from prison and execution. Today, God is still releasing sinners from the prison of sin; and releasing His children from the prison of the enemy's restrictions. The enemy's strategy is to restrict and restrain us from doing the works of Jesus—ministering the Word of God, delivering miracles, and bringing life to people. But ... **there is no power greater than the power of Christ!** His transcendent power is contained and released in our lives whenever we partake of Him through the Meal of His Body and Blood—Passover *and* its corresponding New Testament Meal, Communion.

This Table of Passion that He set for us releases and redeems us from every destructive plan of the enemy. Don't let the enemy hem you in on every side; in fact, don't let the enemy hem you in on any side!

Apprehend Christ's power through His banqueting table!

23. The Fourteenth: A Day of Passion

And they kept the passover on the four-
teenth day...
                    Numbers 9:5

The fourteenth—what a day the fourteenth had become! So many years had passed from the very first Passover in Egypt! The fourteenth of the month certainly had become a day of "passion" on the Hebraic calendar.

Passover represents passion. Passover was the beginning of an ongoing, passionate love affair between God and His people.

You will have songs in the night when you keep
the festival, and gladness of heart...
                    Isaiah 30:29 (NASB)

My beloved is mine, and I am His...
                    Song of Solomon 2:16

Passover was the first Feast that God instituted. Passover was so important to the heart of the Father—and the life of mankind—that it is the *only* Feast God gave a second chance with. If someone could not celebrate Passover on the fourteenth day of the first month, God allowed them to celebrate it on the fourteenth day of the second month;[70] because God is a God of second chances! (Astoundingly, even the Gregorian calendar has a day of "passion" on the fourteenth; the *fourteenth* day of the second month!)

The fourteenth, a day of passion—the day Heaven invested its very Heart for the life of the world.

The fourteenth—the day of Passover. The number fourteen is significant!

> **Fourteen**: double: duplicate; reproduce; recreate; disciple, servant; bond-slave.[71]

Passover, the 14th: God did decide to *double* it—if the first month didn't work, then they could partake of it during the second month.

> *...If any man of you or of your posterity shall be unclean ... yet he shall keep the passover unto the LORD. The fourteenth day of the second month at even they shall keep it...*
> *Numbers 9:10-11*

---

70   Numbers 9:10-11 "Speak unto the children of Israel, saying, If any man of you or of your posterity shall be unclean by reason of a dead body, or be in a journey afar off, yet he shall keep the passover unto the LORD. The fourteenth day of the second month at even they shall keep it, and eat it with unleavened bread and bitter herbs."

71   Ira Milligan, *Understanding the Dreams You Dream* (Shippensburg, PA: Destiny Image Publishers, Inc., 2010), pg. 96.

Passover, the 14th: God did decide to _duplicate_ it. Jesus duplicated the Passover Meal and instituted Communion, _recreating_ the Meal. Remember: He didn't come to "destroy" the law, but to fulfil it.

> _Think not that I am come to destroy the law, or the prophets: I am not come to destroy, but to fulfill._
> _Matthew 5:17_

As Jesus partook of His last Passover on earth, Communion was established. In the passionate _fourteenth_ book of Mark, we see some words worthy of our attention.

> _And as they did eat, Jesus took bread, and blessed, and **brake*** it, and gave to them, and said, Take, eat: this is my body. And he took the cup, and when he had given **thanks****, he gave it to them: and they all drank of it. And he said unto them, This is my blood of the new testament, which is shed for many._
> _Mark 14:22-24_

*Brake: [klao]: used in the NT of the breaking of bread or **communion**.[72]

**Thanks: [eucharisteo].[73]

---

72 Interlinear Concordance, _Blue Letter Bible_, iPhone ed., v. 2.54 (Blue Letter Bible, 2016).

73 Interlinear Concordance, _Blue Letter Bible_, iPhone ed., v. 2.54 (Blue Letter Bible, 2016).

***Eucharist* ...** also called Holy Communion, the Lord's Supper...[74]

Communion, Passover's corresponding *New Testament Meal.*

Passover, the 14th: A day of *disciples,* *servants* and *bond-slaves.* Passover is a day of distinction. Those who are set apart for Him are distinctly His servants.

> *...Moses, the **bond-servant** of God...*
> *Revelation 15:3 (NASB)*

> *Simon Peter, a **bond-servant** and apostle of Jesus Christ...*
> *2 Peter 1:1 (NASB)*

> *James, a **bond-servant** of God and of the Lord Jesus Christ...*
> *James 1:1 (NASB)*

> *Jude, a **bond-servant** of Jesus Christ...*
> *Jude 1:1 (NASB)*

> *Joseph of Arimathaea, being a **disciple** of Jesus...*
> *John 19:38*

> *Now there was at Joppa a certain **disciple** named Tabitha...*
> *Acts 9:36*

---

74   Wikipedia, s.v. "Eucharist." https://en.wikipedia.org/wiki/Eucharist

*...a certain **disciple** was there, named Timotheus...*
Acts 16:1

*Paul, a **bond-servant** of God...*
Titus 1:1 (AMP)

The Revelation of Jesus Christ, which God gave
*... to His **bond-servant** John,*
Revelation 1:1 (NASB)

Jesus, our Passover, had made many disciples and bond-servants (too many to name). Distinctly separate from the world, they were willing to fully surrender to their Passover Lamb—in life or in death!

Passover, the 14th: A day of _reproducing_ (or multiplication). Silver, gold, lands, wealth... Passover continually multiplied their affluence. No sick, no feeble, no lame... Passover continually reproduced their health. As Jesus gave of Himself to His disciples at His last earthly Passover Feast, He was multiplying Himself through them. Becoming more and more like their beloved Master, they now received the authority of His Name. Now, they could "ask the Father in My (Jesus) Name, and He will give it to you."[75] And, even greater— "before they call, I will

---

75   John 16:23 "And in that day ye shall ask me nothing. Verily, verily, I say unto you, Whatsoever ye shall ask the Father in my name, he will give it you."

answer; and while they are yet speaking, I will hear."[76] He had been the *One* doing the works, but they would be the *one(s)* continuing His work.

> ...*whoever believes in me will do the works I have been doing, and they will do even greater things than these, because I am going to the Father.*
> *John 14:12 (NIV)*

Emulating their Teacher, His disciples became disciple-makers. Their disciples would also make disciples. The ever-increasing multiplication still continues. You and I are His present-day disciples with the purpose of God's Kingdom expansion. Now, it is "Christ in *you*, the hope of glory..." (Colossians 1:27).

> *I do not ask on behalf of these alone, but for* **those also who believe in Me through their word**...
> *John 17:20 (NASB)*

> **Of the increase** *of his government* ... **there shall be no end**...
> *Isaiah 9:7*

---

76   Isaiah 65:24 "And it shall come to pass, that before they call, I will answer; and while they are yet speaking, I will hear."

Disciples making disciples! Passover's unwritten rule of release was activated again. The church was birthed, and His Kingdom would forever increase.

24. Release from Serpent's Venom

For as often as ye eat this bread, and drink this
cup, ye do shew the Lord's death till he come.
1 Corinthians 11:26

Sometime after the ascension of Jesus, the Apostle Paul
became a disciple. Then known as Saul, Paul was one of
the most dangerous persecutors of the early Church.

When the Resurrected Lord appeared to Saul on the
road to Damascus, the dramatic conversion of the Apostle
Paul took place. Damascus is a name that means: a sack
full of blood, the similitude of burning.[77] Paul would be
set on fire for God's Kingdom, receiving incredible revelation straight from the Lord Himself on the extraordinary
power in our Passover's blood.

> ***For I have received of the Lord*** *that which*
> *also I delivered unto you, That the Lord Jesus the*
> *same night in which he was betrayed took bread:*
> *And when he had given thanks, he brake it, and*

---

77   SheKnows, s.v. "Damascus," http://www.sheknows.com/baby-names/name/
damascus

said, Take, eat: this is my body, which is broken
for you: this do in remembrance of me.
1 Corinthians 11:23

Chosen and set apart as Christ's vessel, Paul would bear Jesus' name before Gentiles, before kings, and before Israel.[78] Having caused much suffering, he would now suffer much for the name of Jesus Christ.[79] Paul definitely needed revelation on the Blood's power to complete his life's work.

The Lord gave Paul personal instruction on the vital and mysteriously powerful Meal of the Passover Lamb. Receiving revelations, he was the apostle who emphatically declared that…

> *…Christ our passover is sacrificed for us:*
> *1 Corinthians 5:7*

Paul was the apostle who stated…

> *The cup of blessing which we bless, is it not the*
> *communion of the blood of Christ? The bread*
> *which we break, is it not the communion of the*
> *body of Christ?*
> *1 Corinthians 10:16*

---

78   Acts 9:15 "But the Lord said unto him, Go thy way: for he is a chosen vessel unto me, to bear my name before the Gentiles, and kings, and the children of Israel:"

79   Acts 9:16 "For I will shew him how great things he must suffer for my name's sake."

And, Paul is the apostle who stated the importance of eating the Communion Meal of Jesus Christ—often.

> For **as often as** ye eat this bread, and drink this
> cup, ye do shew the Lord's death till he come.
> 1 Corinthians 11:26

Paul knew:

- the *power* released through Passover,
- the *power* of Christ's victory over death and hell,
- the *power* of Christ's Resurrection,

would be *released* "as often as" we partake of Communion's Bread and Wine—the Body and Blood of our Passover Lamb.

Christ gave Paul important revelations of the Cup of Blessing for the new dispensation of grace. Paul released the intense revelations of Communion's power in His writings to the Churches; then demonstrated the power of those revelations in his life's powerful, effective ministry.

Communion became an important, integral part of his life. Consuming the powerful Communion Meal—often—Paul's heart burned passionately for Christ and His blood-purchased church. The church, birthed at the Passover of Heaven's Lamb—birthed in the blood and water that flowed from Christ's side as the soldier's spear was thrust into the very Heart of Heaven! The powerfully passionate apostle forged forward to expand Christ's Kingdom—no matter the risk, no matter the cost. No, saving his life wasn't his first priority—obedience was!

> *...I consider my own life of no importance to me whatsoever, as long as I can finish the course ahead of me, the task I received from the Lord Yeshua...*
> Acts 20:24 (CJB)

He knew the power contained in the Communion Meal because he knew the power contained in Christ!

Paul had come to know the Resurrected Christ, the Glorified One; and, Paul committed himself to being His bond-servant.

> *Paul, a **bond-servant** of God and an apostle ... of Jesus Christ...*
> Titus 1:1 (AMP)

At a literal midnight hour of Paul's day—and a figurative midnight hour of his life—Paul was in the middle of a major storm. As a prisoner, Paul was in a ship going to Rome for trial. Although it was a mighty vessel, their ship was no match for the vicious storm that had flung them about for two weeks as they headed towards Adria. Adria means: darkness. And, dark it was. With no light at all, not even the faintest twinkle of a star, there was no hope of being saved.[80] Those on-board seemed destined for a watery grave.

As a Hebrew, Paul knew what the Israelites did prior to their midnight hour in Egypt—they consumed the Passover Lamb! Paul knew what Jesus did at the coming midnight hour of His life—He consumed the Passover Lamb!

Ironically—or, in perfect synchronicity—it just happened to be near **midnight** on the **fourteenth** day of the storm! Paul knew what He would do! He would *Eucharisteo*. He would partake of the unrivalled, unparalleled, unequivocal power of His Passover Lamb—Jesus Christ. No one had eaten for fourteen days. But...

It was the perfect day—stormy!
It was the perfect time—midnight!
It was the perfect Meal—Bread!

Paul reached passionately for the Bread. He just couldn't help it. It was Jesus' favorite Meal; and it had become his favorite, also.

> *...he took bread, and gave thanks to God in presence of them all: and when he had broken it, he began to eat.*
> *Acts 27:35*

---

80   Acts 27:20 "And when neither sun nor stars in many days appeared, and no small tempest lay on us, all hope that we should be saved was then taken away."

Paul *took* bread. He *lambano* bread. The Greek word [lambano] means: **to take to one's self, to make one's own, of that which when taken is not let go, to seize, apprehend.**[81]

Then, Paul *eucharisteo*, just as Jesus had done. Giving thanks, he knew that Jesus was his Passover! Jesus was his bread. Jesus was his strength and fortitude. Jesus was his life, his all.

Grabbing hold of Heaven's power of release, Paul apprehended Heaven's capacity and ability contained in this tiny, earthly Meal and made it his own. This Bread represented Jesus, and Jesus contains "all the fullness of the Godhead."[82] This Meal holds the potent, dynamic, explosive power of the Supreme Resurrected Christ!

As Paul ate the bread, everyone on the ship was suddenly of "good cheer."[83] They had not yet eaten anything; so, why did Paul's eating of bread make everyone happy? As Paul partook of the *Bread,* a literal shift in the *invisible* realm occurred. External circumstances had not changed. The storm still tossed their boat mercilessly. The sky was still as black as midnight. The waves were just as high.

---

81   Interlinear Concordance, *Blue Letter Bible*, iPhone ed., v. 2.54 (Blue Letter Bible, 2016).

82   Colossians 2:9 "For in him dwelleth all the fulness of the Godhead bodily."

83   Acts 27:36 "Then they were all of good cheer, and they also took some meat."

In fact, things were going to get even worse as their ship would literally be ripped apart[84]—yet they were *all* of good cheer. What was the difference? Heaven's power had been released to move.

As violent waves tore apart their ship, the captain commanded them to swim to shore. Swimming or floating on remains of their ship, every person arrived safely on the island of Melita. Melita is a name that means: affording honey.[85] After all the trauma, the sweetness of solid land beneath their feet certainly made Melita feel like the land of milk and honey. Paul had eaten *bread*; and, in keeping with Passover's custom, escaped was procured!

> *...And so it was that all escaped safely to land.*
> *Acts 27:44 (AMP, parallel Bible)*

Soon after arriving safely on land, Paul encountered a snake.

> *And when Paul had gathered a bundle of sticks,*
> *and laid them on the fire, there came a viper out*
> *of the heat, and fastened on his hand.*
> *Acts 28:3*

---

84   Acts 27:41 "And falling into a place where two seas met, they ran the ship aground; and the forepart stuck fast, and remained unmoveable, but the hinder part was broken with the violence of the waves."

85   SheKnows, s.v. "http://www.sheknows.com/baby-names/name/melita

The islanders expected the worst! All of them expected Paul to die; but, Paul had *eucharisteo*('d) and consumed *artos*. [Artos] means: shewbread,[86] and presence bread.[87] Paul had partaken of Christ! Empowered with Heaven's strength, he was able to shake off the snake.

Paul had eaten the Meal of Remembrance. Paul *remembered* the Lord's death while eating the bread. Paul *remembered* the dethronement of evil powers and the humiliation of hell. Paul *remembered* that satan had been rendered entirely useless and all his works had been completely destroyed. Paul *remembered* that the One Who had all authority in heaven and on earth was "inside" of him.[88] Paul *remembered*!

Once more, it was the enemy who was destroyed—not the one marked with the Blood of the Lamb! Life was written over Paul, deactivating death yet again. With the life of Jesus flowing through his blood, Paul was released from every effect of the enemy's fatal venom. God's power once again superseded earth's natural laws. Soon,

---

86   Interlinear Concordance, *Blue Letter Bible*, iPhone ed., v. 2.54 (Blue Letter Bible, 2016).

87   "Easton's Bible Dictionary," *SwordSearcher*, iPhone ed., v. 3.4 (Brandon Staggs, 1999).

88   Colossians 1:27 "…Christ in you, the hope of glory."

many "came, and were healed"[89] as Paul prayed and laid hands on them. The shipwrecked "prisoner" had come to set them free, *releasing* them from their diseases. Then, the islanders...

> ...*showed us every respect and presented many gifts to us, honoring us with many honors: and when we sailed, they provided and put on board our ship everything we needed.*
> *Acts 28:10 (AMP, parallel Bible)*

Paul knew that his ability to conquer every circumstance and situation was found in Jesus Christ. He didn't just know it—he was convinced.

> ...*I'm absolutely convinced that nothing— nothing living or dead, angelic or demonic, today or tomorrow, high or low, thinkable or unthinkable—absolutely nothing can get between us and God's love because of the way that Jesus our Master has embraced us.*
> *Romans 8:38-39 (MSG)*

Completely convinced, nothing could stop Paul! No shipwreck, no snake, no economy, no government. No! In all these things, he was more than a conqueror—through the One Who loved Him.

---

89   Acts 28:8-9 "And it came to pass, that the father of Publius lay sick of a fever and of a bloody flux: to whom Paul entered in, and prayed, and laid his hands on him, and healed him. So when this was done, others also, which had diseases in the island, came, and were healed:"

*Nay, in all these things we are **more than conquerors** through **him** that loved us.*
Romans 8:37

Jesus' power had once more superseded every force on earth.

*Now thanks be unto God, which always causeth us to triumph **in Christ**...*
2 Corinthians 2:14

Triumph is found in Jesus Christ …Therefore, "in Christ" is exactly where Paul positioned himself.

*He that eateth my flesh … **dwelleth in me**...*
John 6:56

Paul *remembered* that Jesus destroyed[90] all the power of the enemy.[91] Paul's enemy had been … **rendered entirely useless**. Paul positioned himself "in" Christ, and produced much fruit through his effective, powerful, authoritative ministry.

He who abides in Me and I in him, he bears much fruit, for apart from me you can do nothing.
John 15:5 (NASB)

---

90   "Destroy: [*katargeo*]: to render entirely useless."
"Interlinear KJV with Strong's Greek & Hebrew Lexicon," *SwordSearcher*, iPhone ed., v. 3.4
91   Hebrews 2:14 "…that through death he might destroy him that had the power of death, that is, the devil;"

Herein is my Father glorified, that ye bear much fruit...
John 15:8

Will *you* remember? Remember to position yourself in Him by partaking of this vital Meal. Remember the power contained in His Body and Blood. Remember the antidote for the enemy's venom. Remember the dethronement of darkness. Remember His Passion and the triumph of His death. Remember to eat of Him—**often**!

For as often as you do, surely, Heaven's unequivocal power will fill your life and begin to spill over onto those who are around you. You become a channel that releases the power of Heaven—producing much fruit! Watch as faith begins to flicker in the hopeless heart; watch as all begin to be of good cheer! Watch as death gives way to life; watch as sinners are drawn to Christ!

25. Worthily

For he that eateth and drinketh unworthily…
1 Corinthians 11:29

Fear has caused many of God's children to miss out on the Table of the Lord's Supper. We are doing ourselves a great disfavor if we do not partake of this powerfully potent Meal. The enemy does everything in his power to keep us from consuming the Body and Blood of the One Who so violently overthrew his power. Satan understands the power contained in this Meal because it has terminated his plans, time and time again!

So, how can we eat and drink *worthily?* Who could be worthy to partake of a meal of such great value, a meal priced at the life of the very Son of God?

Scripture says that if we eat and drink *unworthily,* we will be guilty of the Body and Blood of the Lord.[92] We know that if we drink *unworthily,* we drink damnation to

---

92   1 Corinthians 11:27 "Wherefore whosoever shall eat this bread, and drink this cup of the Lord, unworthily, shall be guilty of the body and blood of the Lord."

ourselves;[93] and, "For this cause many are weak and sickly among you, and many sleep" (1 Corinthians 11:30).

Fear stems from these verses in 1 Corinthians when we don't have a proper understanding of them. But when we start understanding the original Greek words of these verses, we gain a deeper understanding of the Lord's Supper. Let's take a closer look at the requirements, or pre-requisites, of partaking of the Body and Blood of our Lord.

In the Old Testament, God (through Moses) stated the requirements that had to be met in order to eat the Passover Meal. These requirements also apply to the New Testament Lord's Supper of Communion.

> *And the LORD said unto Moses and Aaron,*
> *This is the ordinance of the passover: There shall*
> *no stranger eat thereof:*
> *Exodus 12:43*

In this verse, *stranger* is the Hebrew words [ben] [nekar] meaning: son of a foreigner. It wasn't only Israelites that partook of the Passover Meal. They had foreigners and hired servants that ate of it. If foreigners participated in Passover with the Israelites, then what does "son of a foreigner" actually mean?

---

93   1 Corinthians 11:29 "For he that eateth and drinketh unworthily, eateth and drinketh damnation to himself, not discerning the Lord's body."

There was a requirement that, when met, allowed one to move from "stranger" to "partaker." That requirement was circumcision! Circumcision was a sign of blood covenant. When the son of a foreigner joined with the Israelites, the rite of circumcision permitted and entitled him to the benefits and advantages of an Israelite. They were then treated as a "son."

> *Any slave you have bought may eat it after you have circumcised him,*
> *Exodus 12:44 (NIV)*

> *And when a stranger shall sojourn with thee, and will keep the passover to the LORD, let all his males be circumcised, and then let him come near and keep it; and **he shall be as one that is born in the land**...*
> *Exodus 12:48*

In the New Testament, there is a different form of circumcision. It is the circumcision of the heart!

> *...**true circumcision is circumcision of the heart**, by the Spirit, not by the fulfillment of the letter of the Law...*
> *Romans 2:29 (AMP)*

> *Moreover the LORD your God **will circumcise your heart**, and the heart of your descendants, to love the LORD your God with all your heart, and with all your soul, so that you may live.*
> *Deuteronomy 30:6 (NASB)*

This circumcision is a literal change of heart as God cuts away our carnal nature. When we believe in Jesus Christ as Lord and confess Him as Saviour, we become "sons" of Abraham. God, Himself, circumcises our hearts, meeting His requirement of blood covenant. We go from being a "son of a foreigner" to being a "son of promise." We become sons and daughters of the Living God.

> So ***if you belong to Christ, you are now part of Abraham's family***, *and you will be given what God has promised.*
> *Galatians 3:29 (CEV)*

> *Behold, what manner of love the Father hath bestowed upon us, that we should be called the* ***sons of God…***
> *1 John 3:1*

As a "son of God," we are no longer the "son of a foreigner." As a "son of God" we are *worthy*—in the aspect of being righteous—to participate in the Love Feast that Jesus has set for us. (It is not dependent on our ability to be perfect. We are unable to attain perfection without the Blood of Jesus.)

When His Blood is applied to our hearts, then, as we discussed earlier in chapter 16, we are justified—"**declared to be entitled to all the advantages and rewards arising from perfect obedience**." We are now *worthy* because we have received the perfection of Christ's righteousness. We are purified and cleansed. It is based on His righteousness. **This is a Table that is set for believers**.

Since Paul was addressing *believers* in Corinth, what does "unworthily" actually mean?

Unworthily is the Greek word [anaxios] which means: irreverently.[94] (As discussed previously, only the Blood of Christ makes us worthy—only the Blood!) But we can, and must, examine ourselves to make sure that we eat of Communion *reverently*. This does not allude to eating of it in a stringent, rigid, or fearful way. Revere really means: to hold in high esteem, be awed by, adore. The cost that Christ has paid to prepare this Meal denotes that it is a Meal worthy of esteem and honor. It is a Meal to be cherished and treasured, held in the highest regard.

Revere also means: lionize. This means: to celebrate, honor, applaud and exalt. This implies characteristics of a *joyful* feast. Communion is a Feast to be celebrated! In the New Testament era, Communion became known as the *Agape Love Feast*. Paul wonderfully drew an analogy between Passover and our Agape Love Feast. He also stated that *as many times as* we eat the Communion Feast we show the Lord's death. Every time we partake of the Feast of His Passion, we must do it with reverence

---

94   "Interlinear KJV with Strong's Greek & Hebrew Lexicon," *SwordSearcher*, iPhone ed., v. 3.4

and respect, celebrating the infinite price Christ paid to serve us this Meal—and the unequalled sacrifice He gave because of love.

The opposite of revere is: despise. **We must not take for granted or lack respect for the cost He has paid, the war He has won, and the Passion He has poured out!**

We have the responsibility to partake worthily—with reverence, with high esteem for the unparalleled Meal He has served. It is His Priceless Body and His Incomparable Blood that we are consuming; and we must not disdain it. His sacrifice must always be regarded with due respect and fear. Not fear as in *afraid*; but, fear as in *the reverential fear of the Lord.*

The Lord God prophesied through Isaiah about Feasts consumed (Passover included), and sacrifices made, without the right heart attitude.

> To what purpose is the multitude of your sac-
> rifices to me [unless they are the offering of the
> heart]? says the Lord...
>   Isaiah 1:11 (AMP, parallel Bible)

When we partake of this Holy Meal, we must do it from the depths of our hearts, delighting and rejoicing in the wondrous gift(s) He has given us ... always in remembrance of Him.

What good would it do to partake of this **passionately powerful Feast** without regarding the **powerfully passionate One**?

The answer is ... "Nothing!"

Unbelief does not change the power of Jesus Christ; it simply prevents us from experiencing that power. Therefore, without regard for the One Who is the substance of the Meal, the power contained in the Meal is simply not apprehended.

In the book of Jude, we see the writer speaking of the *feasts of charity* while also making a very obvious and powerful connection to the Passover. He begins with Paul's wording—*remembrance*.

> *I will therefore put you in remembrance, though ye once knew this, how that the Lord, having saved the people out of the land of Egypt...*
>
> *Jude 1:5*

We see reference made to the Feasts of Charity, or Love Feasts. And there were spots, or blemishes, in these Agape Love Feasts.

> *These are spots in your **feasts of charity**, when they feast with you, <u>feeding themselves without fear</u>: clouds they are without water, carried about*

of winds; trees whose fruit withereth, without
fruit, twice dead, plucked up by the roots;
Jude 1:12

Again, we see that some in the Church were participating in the Love Feast without the right heart attitude.

The result of eating improperly is:

- emptiness,
- lack of direction,
- perishing (withering) of fruit,
- no fruit,
- no life,
- and dead roots —**absolutely no effectiveness**!

Eating improperly caused all power contained in this powerful Feast to be rendered ineffective in their lives.

We must learn to discern the Lord's Body!

26. Learn to Discern

...not discerning the Lord's body. For this cause many are weak and sickly among you, and many sleep.
1 Corinthians 11:29-30

The Church of Corinth was small, having many weak and sickly members. In contrast, the millions of Israel did not have one feeble person among them.

> Here are two bodies of people: one in the Old Testament, the other in the New Testament. One under law, the other under grace. One under a covenant based on the blood of animals, the other under the covenant of the blood of the Son of God ... Surely something was lacking at Corinth, and something is still lacking where such conditions exist.
> —T.L. Osborn

We need to discern the Lord's Body and Blood. Believers, who didn't need to die, have died because we didn't properly discern the Lord's body. It is of utmost importance that we learn to discern!

His **body** *bore* our sins, His **body** *heals* our diseases. [95] His **blood** *forgives* and *eradicates* our sins;[96] His **blood** *cleanses* our consciences.[97] When we don't *discern* (recognize and perceive) what the Body and Blood of the Lord has done for us, then Communion does us no good. Its power is rendered ineffective in our lives—therefore sickness and weakness can come upon us.

We MUST learn to discern the Lord's body!

> Sickness is due to the failure of being taught about the body of Christ as we have been taught about the blood of Christ.
> —T.L. Osborn

In Egypt, on that fateful yet miraculous night, there was lambs' blood everywhere. What made the difference between Egypt's fate and Israel's miracles?

> Every Israelite who put the lamb's blood on the doorpost was protected from the destroyer who brought death. Every Israelite who ate the lamb's body was freed from sickness and made well, strong, and healthy.
> —T.L. Osborn

---

95   1 Peter 2:24 "Who his own self bare our sins in his own body on the tree… by whose stripes ye were healed"

96   Hebrews 9:22 "…without shedding of blood is no remission."

97   Hebrews 9:14 "How much more shall the blood of Christ…purge your conscience from dead works…"

Even if the Egyptians had started applying lamb's blood all over their homes, they still would *not* have been saved. They did not have the understanding of how to apply the blood or partake of the lamb. They did not understand what the lamb's body and blood could, and would, do. Just splashing blood haphazardly over their homes would *not* have been effective; it would *not* have delivered them from the pending destruction!

On the other hand, flinging around lambs' blood *would **not** have caused the death* of their eldest sons. (The destroyer delivered the blow!) Therefore, receiving Communion improperly does not cause death; *but ...* **its power to deliver from judgment and danger is rendered ineffective,** *leaving us vulnerable to the plan of the enemy.*

The power in the blood must be apprehended. Egypt was *ignorant* of Passover's ability to deliver them from the death angel. Again: when we don't perceive, or discern, what the Lord's body has done for us, then Communion does us no good; therefore, judgment or curse can come upon us. So, we see that *discern*-ment is **necessary!**

Let's look at the Greek words in the phrase, "Discern the Lord's Body."

1. **Discern** the Lord's Body!

DISCERN: *Discern* is the Greek word [diakrino] which means: to make a distinction.

Sounds exactly like what Passover was about. *"I will make a clear distinction between my people and your people..."* God made a clear and obvious distinction; now, we must make a clear and obvious distinction—choosing Christ over the things of this world.

Is it obvious that we belong to Him?

> <u>Remember:</u> ...our faith is the *only* instrument by which the soul appropriates or apprehends Christ and His righteousness.

> <u>But:</u> ...Good works, while not the ground, are the *certain consequence* of justification.[98]

Good works don't save us—*but,* they are a *certain consequence* of our faith. Consequence means: result or outcome. Therefore, good works are a *certain* (known for sure, established beyond a doubt) result of our faith.

Faith without works is dead.[99] Our lives should be *distinctly* different from those who don't belong to Christ!

Furthermore, *discern* comes from the root word [krino] meaning: approve, esteem, prefer. So, we can also say,

---

98   "Easton's Bible Dictionary," *SwordSearcher*, iPhone ed., v. 3.4 (Brandon Staggs, 1999).

99   James 2:17 "Even so faith, if it hath not works, is dead, being alone." James 2:20 "But wilt thou know, O vain man, that faith without works is dead?" James 2:26 "For as the body without the spirit is dead, so faith without works is dead also."

"Approve, esteem and prefer the Lord's Body!" above all else.

2. Discern the **Lord's** Body!

LORD: The Greek word for *Lord* in 1 Corinthians 11:29 is [kurios] meaning: supreme in authority.

Remember: through death—the overpowering of it— Jesus became the ruling authority of all.

> *...he is ... the firstborn from the dead:* ***that in all things he might have the preeminence.***
> *Colossians 1:18*

Again, pre-eminence is the fact of surpassing all others. The supremacy of His Kingship had been sealed! The supremacy of His authority had been secured! All power in heaven and on earth had been given to Him.

> *...All power is given unto me in heaven and in earth.*
> *Matthew 28:18*

3. Discern the Lord's **Body**!

BODY: *Body* is the Greek word [soma] meaning: that which casts a shadow as distinguished from the shadow itself.[100]

---

100 Interlinear Concordance, *Blue Letter Bible*, iPhone ed., v. 2.54 (Blue Letter Bible, 2016).

A shadow is an imperfect image resembling the real thing which casts it. It is an imperfect copy of the perfect real image.
—Julia Blum

The word [soma] makes it clear that Christ's physical body was the **real perfect image** that cast the shadow of Old Testament.

Important note: In another aspect, **the Lord's "Body" is also His Church**! He is the head—we are the body...

*...he is the head of **the body, the church**...*
Colossians 1:18

*...**you are Christ's body**, and individually members of it.*
1 Corinthians 12:27 (NASB)

If the Church is His body, we must also [krino]— *approve, esteem* and *prefer*—each other. This is exactly what Christ has asked of us.

*...let each **esteem** other better than themselves.*
Philippians 2:3

*...give **preference** to one another...*
Romans 12:10 (NASB)

Honoring and esteeming each other is part of discerning the Lord's Body.

Body [soma] comes from the word [sozo]. Sozo is a perfect description of what His *flesh* body accomplished for His *Church* body.

Sozo means:

> **keep safe and sound,**
> **to rescue from danger or destruction,**
> **to save a suffering one (from perishing),**
> **to save one suffering from disease,**
> **to make well,**
> **heal,**
> **restore to health,**
> **to preserve one who is in danger**
> **of destruction.**[101]

Sozo also means...

> **to deliver from the penalties of the**
> **Messianic judgment,**
> **to save from the evils that**
> **obstruct the reception of the**
> **Messianic deliverance.**[102]

This is what His Body and Blood does for us!!

---

101 Interlinear Concordance, *Blue Letter Bible*, iPhone ed., v. 2.54 (Blue Letter Bible, 2016).

102 Interlinear Concordance, *Blue Letter Bible*, iPhone ed., v. 2.54 (Blue Letter Bible, 2016).

His *Body* holds our deliverance from sin's devastation and destruction! His *Cup* holds our deliverance from sin and its all-encompassing guilt.

Have you discerned the unrivalled ability of Jesus' Body to keep you safe, to rescue you from danger, to heal and restore? Have you discerned the unrivalled power of His Body to deliver you from judgment and save you from evil? Have you recognized Jesus as the supreme authority? May you perceive His pre-eminence—His unsurpassed capabilities! **He alone is the One Who delivers us from penalties and evil.**

27. No Fear

*The LORD is the portion of my inheritance and
of my cup...*
Psalm 16:5 (NASB)

Portion is the Greek word [manah] meaning: to prepare
and appoint. The Lord truly did *prepare* a Cup for me! It
is a Cup that overflows with inheritance and blessings. As
I consume this Cup, I honor the One Who prepared it at
a great price.

*What shall I render unto the LORD for all
his benefits toward me? I will take the **cup**
of salvation...*
Psalm 116:12-13

The Communion Cup of His Blood is our Cup of
Blessing. The Greek word for *cup* is the word [poterion]
which comes from the word [peno] meaning...

**to receive into the soul what serves to
refresh, strengthen, nourish it unto
life eternal.**[103]

---

103 Interlinear Concordance, *Blue Letter Bible*, iPhone ed., v. 2.54
(Blue Letter Bible, 2016).

As we take the Cup, we apprehend the power of Christ's eternal life! This is why satan wants us to be afraid of receiving the Communion Meal, always making us fear weakness, sickness, and death. He is our accuser, constantly reminding us of our sins and shortcomings. He wants us to think that Communion will cause our demise; but ... this Cup is full of the refreshment, strength, and nourishment of eternal life; not death! Again, if eaten improperly, **Communion's power to deliver is not apprehended**—leaving us open to sickness, leaving us open to death, leaving us open to the destruction of the enemy, and leaving us vulnerable to the one who *will* steal, kill, and destroy. It is not God Who causes death, but the enemy.

> *Through faith he kept the passover, and the sprinkling of blood,* ***lest he that destroyed ... should touch them.***
> *Hebrews 11:28*

There is a destroyer...

> *...the angel from the bottomless pit; his name in Hebrew is Abaddon, and in Greek, Apollyon—* ***the Destroyer.***
> *Revelation 9:11 (NLT)*

Jesus came to give us life!

> *...I am come that they might have life, and that they might have it more abundantly.*
> *John 10:10*

Jesus is not afraid of sin; He came to save the sinner. He faced sin head-on and brought us salvation.

> *And she shall bring forth a son, and thou shalt call his name JESUS: for **he shall save his people from their sins.***
> *Matthew 1:21*

Once our sins are under the blood of Jesus Christ, they are gone forever. The blood of Jesus is more powerful than *any* sin. The blood of Jesus is more powerful than *every* sin.[104]

> *...for I will forgive their iniquity, and I will remember their sin no more.*
> *Jeremiah 31:34*

> The blood of Jesus is the greatest mystery of eternity, the deepest mystery of divine wisdom.[105]
> —Andrew Murray

---

104 Wendy Varga, *Sacred Secret* (Victoria, BC: FriesenPress, 2017), pg. 41.

105 Andrew Murray, *The Power of the Blood of Jesus* (Blacksburg, VA: Wilder Publications, 2001), pg. 12. ISBN 10:1-61720-275-9.

Jesus does not cause death; He delivers us from death.

> *Who delivered us from so great a death, and doth deliver...*
> *2 Corinthians 1:10*

Moses and the Israelites kept the first Passover *with faith*, and the destroyer was deactivated. So, too, we must keep the Lord's Supper *with faith*, apprehending all the unequalled, unrivalled power of Heaven that **renders the "destroyer" entirely useless.**

Choose to become a *son of commandment* and choose to partake of the body and lifeblood of our Resurrected Christ. Apprehend the power of His life. Christ will flow through you, empowering you with obedience and the strength to overcome!

> *Now unto him that is able to keep you from falling, and to present you faultless before the presence of his glory with exceeding joy,*
> *Jude 1:24*

Jesus is our Passover! Let us feast on Him with reverence and honor! He is the One worthy of all glory and blessing, the One worthy of all power and authority, the One worthy to receive the reward for His suffering!

172

28. Keep the Feast

Therefore let us keep the feast...
1 Corinthians 5:8

When Paul wrote to the Church in Rome, he made a very thought-provoking statement. Paul said,

...death reigned from Adam to Moses...
Romans 5:14

What?! Why did Paul say "Moses"—and not "Jesus"? Paul said that death ran rampant throughout the earth until the time of *Moses*. What happened during Moses' era that changed the power that death had enjoyed since Adam's fall?

During Moses' generation:

- ***Passover's Meal*** *was instituted.*
- ***Passover's Blood*** *was applied.*
- ***Passover's Lamb*** *was eaten.*

During the time of Moses, Israel began to partake of the Passover Lamb. For the first time ever, the Passover Lamb was slain and consumed. (Not just any lamb—but the *PASSOVER LAMB*).

During the time of Moses, they began to eat of—and apprehend—a power that had not been touched before! **They began to eat a Meal *impregnated with the very power of Heaven*!** They began to eat the Passover Lamb, the...

> *...Lamb slain from the foundation of the world.*
> *Revelation 13:8*

They began to eat...

> *...spiritual meat:*
> *1 Corinthians 10:3*

They began to drink...

> *...spiritual drink: for they drank of ... Christ.*
> *1 Corinthians 10:4*

Jesus—the real and perfect Passover Lamb—had not yet been slain on the earth; but, **in the spiritual realm, the death of the Holy Lamb of God had already happened!** Passover signified what was yet to occur in earth's sphere.

During the time of Moses, mankind began to consume the *shadow* of Jesus' body; then, death—for the first time ever—could not reign.

The consuming of *life* had begun! The flesh of the Lamb was consumed, and the lifeblood of the Lamb was applied! Death could no longer rule. Death could no longer go wherever he wanted to go, enter wherever he wanted to enter, or do whatever he wanted to do. For the first time ever, the destroyer had been turned away. The Lord did...

> ...*not allow the destroyer to come into your houses to slay you.*
> *Exodus 12:23 (AMP)*

And the Lord...

> ...*smote the Egyptians, but spared our homes...*
> *Exodus 12:27 (NASB)*

The great Psalmist of Israel, King David, sang about a table that the Lord had prepared for us in the presence of our enemies (Psalm 23:5). King David would have grown up hearing about the passionately powerful stories of Passover. He knew Heaven's potential was contained in a mysteriously powerful Meal that was eaten in the enemy's presence time and time again.

Passover certainly had been prepared and served right in the very midst of the enemy; and **with every consumption of this Meal, the forces of evil took a deadly, devastating blow**.

In all its power and force, Passover was a *shadow* of the New Testament Meal's reality. The Lamb, the Bread, the Wine were all potent symbols of the One Who was to come. For the Old Testament was…

> …*a shadow of good things to come, and not the very image of the things*…
> *Hebrews 10:1*

> Remember: A shadow is an imperfect image resembling the real thing which casts it. It is an imperfect copy of the perfect real image.
> —Julia Blum

The Old Testament was a shadow. Christ is the perfect, real image!

> …*in respect to a festival … things which are a mere shadow of what is to come; but **the substance belongs to Christ**.*
> *Colossians 2:16-17 (NASB)*

The true substance of Passover's Feast is Jesus Christ!

Consumption of the *shadow* was potently powerful; how much more so consumption of the *real, perfect image*!

We cannot add to what He has fully accomplished on our behalf ... You can do nothing! You can add nothing! All you can do is drink it! All you can do is receive it! All you can do is believe it! Believe it and enjoy it!
—Justin Abraham

The way to do battle is to sit and "Feast!" The Feasts are reminders of victory; and, the Feasts are seasons of breakthrough! The Feast of Communion is connected with the Feast of Passover! And every time we Feast on Jesus Christ, we literally terrorize the hordes of hell. We strike absolute panic into the hearts of our enemies, as we ...

...do shew the Lord's death...
1 Corinthians 11:26

Communion is the act that causes sheer terror to the forces of darkness as they watch us partake and legally and officially declare into that realm the law of Jesus' death. We *put into effect* the very law that destroyed the devil's power and his works. [106]

Every Sabbath and every holiday, the Jewish people are to *remember* going out of Egypt. In fact, they have a commandment to remember leaving Egypt **every day**.

Jesus Christ is our Passover! What would happen if we would *remember* to partake of our Passover Lamb—Jesus

---

106 Wendy Varga, *Sacred Secret* (Victoria, BC: FriesenPress, 2017), pg. 24.

Christ—*daily*, and *remember* His unparalleled powers?! **With every consumption of this Meal, hell's forces take a deadly, devastating blow** and the very power of God to save is released.

29. Power for Your Midnight Hour

Don't face your midnight without the power of this Meal! In your deadest, darkest night ... feast on life!

Are you in the bondage of Egypt or trapped in wilderness wanderings? Are you standing at the impassable walls of your Jericho, feeling helpless, hopeless, and defeated?

> ➤ **Consume the One Who is your Deliverer!**

Are you standing at death's door, ravaged with sickness and disease? Is the serpent's venom coursing through your body?

> ➤ **Eat of the Giver of Life!**

Is your soul full of trauma and pain? Is your mind oppressed by demonic forces?

> ➤ **Drink His Cup of Blessing!**

Is the enemy wreaking havoc with your family? Is destruction passing through your marriage, home, or business?

> ➤ **Now is the Time for Passover!**

Are you in the blackness of a deadly storm? Are you held behind prison bars of suffocating restrictions?

> ➤ **Break some Bread and Give Thanks!**

Are you standing on the brink of your destiny, looking for more power, authority, and effectiveness? Are you needing to know Him more intimately?

> ➤ **Keep the Feast!**

All the power, all the force, all the potency, all the strength of Passover's mere shadow is contained and exceeded in the covenant Communion Meal.

This isn't just any lamb—this is God's Passover Lamb!
This isn't just a shadow—this is reality!
This isn't just a ritual—this is life!

Consume the Lamb and His Blood! Eat a Meal saturated and drenched with Heaven's power! As you do, Jesus will be established in your life and home! Agape's Love Feast releases His essential power of renewal! Jesus—the essence of life and love.

With a new-found depth of revelation and love for His Covenant Meal, may overwhelming exuberance to celebrate His Love Feast fill the very core of your being!

Go ahead! Keep the Feast! Feast on the One Who is above all in supremacy! Feast on Agape Love Himself! You are His betrothed, His beloved! You are bought with a price—the price of our Passover Lamb's precious blood!

So, go ahead! Pick up the Bread and take hold of the Cup! Consume Him yet once more! Heaven's mysterious, unrivalled capacity contained and served in one earthly meal will be your turning point! Heaven's power is about to be released into you!

****

Jesus Christ—He is the power in the Meal.

...Christ the power of God...
1 Corinthians 1:24

Jesus Christ—He is the mystery in the Meal.

...God's mystery, that is, Christ Himself.
Colossians 2:2 (NASB)

****

Start right now... Release the power of Jesus—the power that supersedes every power on earth! Jesus for Passover, and all year round! *HE* is the mystery of all mysteries! *HE* is your ultimate Feast!

What will your tomorrow hold?

Only insofar as you eat and drink flesh and blood, the flesh and blood of the Son of Man, do you have life within you. The one who brings a hearty appetite to this eating and drinking has eternal life and will be fit and ready for the Final Day. My flesh is real food and my blood is real drink. By eating my flesh and drinking my blood you enter into me and I into you. In the same way that the fully alive Father sent me here and I live because of him, so the one who makes a meal of me lives because of me. This is the Bread from heaven. Your ancestors ate bread and later died. Whoever eats this Bread will live always.

—JESUS CHRIST
John 6:53-58 (MSG)

ENEMY TO MY ENEMIES

Wendy Varga

Just like You told the Israelite children,
Just like You said to Moses, Your man,
Your Word's still in the air for You are the Great I AM.

Chorus:
You are enemy to my enemies,
Adversary to my adversaries.
You are enemy to my enemies,
Adversary to my adversaries.

So, Lion of Judah, scatter the enemy,
Lion of Judah, gather Your sons.
Your roar's still in the air for You are the Righteous One.

Bridge:
So roar, Mighty Lion; roar, Mighty Lion.
Lion of Judah, bring us new hope,
Your sound strikes fear and terror
Right up into the enemies' throats.

I LAUGH

Wendy Varga

Chorus:
I laugh (ha-ha), I laugh (uh, huh)
For victory is mine.
I laugh (ha-ha), I laugh (uh, huh)
The enemy's defeated.
I laugh (ha-ha), I laugh (uh, huh)
For victory is mine,
and there's power in the blood of Jesus.

No weapon formed against me shall prosper,
And fiery darts must fall down to the ground.
I triumph in the blood of Jesus,
And in His blood deliverance is found.

Satan thought that he had won the battle,
As in death, Jesus' head fell down and bowed.
But Christ showed up in hell's deep, ugly dungeon,
And captivity itself was finally bound.

COMMANDER-IN-CHIEF

Wendy Varga

Chorus:
Commander-in-Chief of the army of the Living God,
Commander-in-Chief of the army, unite us as one.
Open our eyes that we may see all You want us to,
Open our ears that we may hear Your words strong and true.
For with justice You judge, with justice You make war,
Commander-in-Chief of the army, the army of the Lord.
Commander-in-Chief.

Your eyes are flames of fire
On Your head are many crowns
From Your mouth comes a sword
And Your name is Lord of Lords,
Commander-in-Chief.

You stroll among the lampstands
Your hand holds the stars
No one is worthy to open the scroll
But the perfect Son of God,
Commander-in-Chief.

CORONATION DAY

Wendy Varga

I want to have a Coronation Day for you, Jesus!
As my voice I raise,
Let this be a Coronation Day for you, Jesus!
I want to crown you with my praise.

Chorus:
Worthy is the Lamb that was slain
To receive power and riches and wisdom and strength,
And honor and glory and blessing.

Bridge:
Blessed be Your Name,
Blessed be the Lamb that was slain.
Blessed be Your Name, Jesus!

ABOUT THE AUTHOR

Wendy Varga ministers at *Portal of Glory Christian Ministries International,* which was founded by her parents—Moses and Rosemary Sabo—in Edmonton, AB, Canada. Portal of Glory was founded with a vision to build a house worthy of God's presence, a house where He can move freely. A significant part of our vision is to equip God's people, preparing them to fulfill God's purpose for their lives.

The purpose is that, through the church, the multifaceted wisdom of God might be made known [revealing the mystery] to the [angelic] rulers and authorities in the heavenly places. (See Ephesians 3:10).

Wendy has a deep passion for the nations, longing to see "The kingdoms of this world are become the kingdoms of our Lord, and of his Christ; and he shall reign for ever and ever." (Revelation 11:15). "Ask for the nations" resounds throughout her being! She carries a deep love for Israel in her heart along with a call to bring the heart of the Church toward Israel.

The power of communion and worship has become a first priority and focal point in her ministry to the Church. Her desire is to see the very heartbeat of God pulsate in the worship of His Bride and for the Warrior Bride of our Beloved to have an intimate and deep revelation of the power and worth of His Body and Blood.

REFERENCES

ALL QUOTATIONS USED WITH PERMISSION

Abraham, Justin Paul. *Grace + Life with Justin Paul Abraham | Tribe Session One*, produced by Company of Burning Hearts. March 27, 2017. Podcast, MP3 audio, 1:06:45. https://www.podomatic.com/podcasts/companyofburninghearts/episodes/2017-03-27T07_58_49-07_00

"Acquiring rights to land by way of prescription." *TCY Legal Chit Chat.* http://www.tcyoung.co.uk/blog/2012/commercial/acquiring-rights-to-land-by-way-of-prescription

"Anamnesis (Christianity)." Wikipedia. https://en.wikipedia.org/wiki/Anamnesis_(Christianity)

"Bar and Bat Mitzvah." Wikipedia. https://en.wikipedia.org/wiki/Bar_and_Bat_Mitzvah

Blum, Julia. "In God's Image." *Israel Institute of Biblical Studies.* https://lp.israelbiblicalstudies.com/lp_iibs_biblical_hebrew_tzel_tzelem-en.html

Cahn, Jonathan. *The Book of Mysteries.* (Lake Mary, FL: FrontLine, 2016.), pg. 199. Used by permission

"Easton's Bible Dictionary." *SwordSearcher.* iPhone ed., v, 3.4. Brandon Staggs, 1999.

"Eucharist." Wikipedia. https://en.wikipedia.org/wiki/Eucharist

"Interlinear Concordance." *Blue Letter Bible.* V. 2.54. Blue Letter Bible, 2016. iOS 7.0 or later.

Milligan, Ira. *Understanding the Dreams You Dream*. Shippensburg, PA: Destiny Image Publishers, Inc., 2010.

Murray, Andrew. *The Power of the Blood of Jesus*. (Blacksburg, VA: Wilder Publications, 2001). pg. 12. ISBN 10:1-61720-275-9

New Oxford American Dictionary. Oxford: Oxford University Press, 2010.

Osborn, T. L. *Healing the Sick: A Living Classic.* Tulsa, OK: Harrison House Inc., 1992. http://www.mimi-huayuan.net/wp-content/uploads/2014/09/Healing-the-Sick_-A-Living-Clas-T.-L.-Osborn.pdf

Oxford American Writer's Thesaurus. Oxford: Oxford University Press, 2010.

"Prescription: Legal Deadlines." *Éducaloi.* https://www.educaloi.qc.ca/en/capsules/prescription-legal-deadlines

SheKnows, s.v. "Damascus," http://www.sheknows.com/baby-names/name/damascus

SheKnows, s.v. "Melita," http://www.sheknows.com/baby-names/name/melita

The Free Dictionary, s.v. "prescription," http://legal-dictionary.thefreedictionary.com/prescription

Varga, Wendy. *Sacred Secret*. Victoria, BC: FriesenPress, 2017.

Whiston, William. Taken from *Josephus The Complete Works,* by William Whiston, A.M., 1998. Nashville, TN: Thomas Nelson Publishers, pg. 576. Used by permission of Thomas Nelson. www.thomasnelson.com.

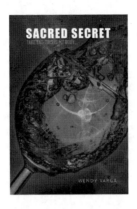